THE AMERICAN KENNEL CLUB'S
Meet the
Chihuahua™

The Responsible Dog Owner's Handbook

AKC's
Meet the Breeds
Series

I-5
EST 2013
PRESS

Irvine, California
A Division of
I-5 Publishing, LLC

AN OFFICIAL PUBLICATION OF   AKC   THE AMERICAN KENNEL CLUB

AMERICAN
KENNEL CLUB

Brought to you by The American Kennel Club and The Chihuahua Club of America.
Vice President, Chief Content Officer: June Kikuchi
Vice President, Kennel Club Books: Andrew DePrisco
Lead Editor: Karen Julian
Art Director: Cindy Kassebaum
Production Manager: Laurie Panaggio
Production Supervisor: Jessica Jaensch
Production Coordinator: Leah Rosalez

Photographs by: Blackhawk Productions (Dwight Dyke): 117; Cheryl Ertelt: 4, 14-15, 30, 40, 50, 54, 58-59, 85, 121; Christopher Appoldt Photography: 56; Close Encounters of the Furry Kind (Jeannie Harrison): 3, 22, 23, 43, 44, 55, 71, 109; Fox Hill Photo: Daniel Johnson, 53, 77; Paulette Johnson, 27, 39, 63, 78-79, 86, 90, 92, 97, 100; Connie Summers/Paulette Johnson, 38, 82, 83; Gina Cioli/BowTie Studio: 4, 68, 80, 91; José Alberto Christiansen: Cover insets, 4, 9, 10, 16, 18-19, 26, 33, 34, 60, 62, 64, 65, 72, 73, 75, 84, 113, 115, 118; LMEimages (Laurie Meehan-Elmer): 42, 46, 81, 93, 94, 102, 107, 110-111; Mark Raycroft Photography: Cover insets, 1, 4, 6-7, 11, 13, 17, 20, 21, 24-25, 29, 32, 35, 36-37, 41, 47, 48-49, 51, 52, 57, 61, 66-67, 69, 76, 88-89, 98-99, 103, 104, 108, 114; Shutterstock: Cover, Back cover, 12, 70, 87, 95, 96, 116, 119, 120, 124; Sporthorse Photography (Tara Gregg): 101, 112

I-5 Press
Division of I-5 Publishing, LLC
3 Burroughs, Irvine, CA 92618

Library of Congress Cataloging-in-Publication Data

The American Kennel Club's meet the Chihuahua : the responsible dog owner's handbook.
    p. cm. -- (AKC's meet the breeds series)
  "Brought to you by The American Kennel Club and The Chihuahua Club of America."
  Includes bibliographical references and index.
  ISBN 978-1-937049-97-3
 1. Chihuahua (Dog breed) I. American Kennel Club. II. Chihuahua Club of America. III. Title: Meet the Chihuahua.
  SF429.C45A44 2012
  636.76--dc23
                                        2012017881

Printed and bound in the United States
15 14 13   3 4 5 6 7 8 9 10

Meet Your New Dog

Welcome to *Meet the Chihuahua*. Whether you're a long-time Chihuahua owner, or you've just gotten your first puppy, we wish you a lifetime of happiness and enjoyment with your new pet.

In this book, you'll learn about the history of the breed, receive tips on feeding, grooming, and training, and learn about all the fun you can have with your dog. The American Kennel Club and BowTie Press hope that this book serves as a useful guide on the lifelong journey you'll take with your canine companion.

Owned and cherished by millions across America, Chihuahuas make wonderful companions and also enjoy taking part in a variety of dog sports, including Conformation (dog shows), Obedience, Rally®, and Agility.

Thousands of Chihuahuas have also earned the AKC Canine Good Citizen® certification by demonstrating their good manners at home and in the community. We hope that you and your Chihuahua will become involved in AKC events, too! Learn how to get involved at www.akc .org/events or find a training club in your area at www.akc.org/events/trainingclubs.cfm.

We encourage you to connect with other Chihuahua owners on the AKC website (www .akc.org), Facebook (www.facebook.com /americankennelclub), and Twitter (@akcdoglovers). Also visit the website for the Chihuahua Club of America (www.chihuahua clubofamerica.com), the national parent club for the Chihuahua, to learn about the breed from reputable exhibitors and breeders.

Enjoy *Meet the Chihuahua*!

Sincerely,

Dennis B. Sprung
AKC President and CEO

14

48

78

88

Contents

CHAPTER ONE

Small Dog, Big Heart

There is *mucho* machismo in this little puppy! The pint-sized Chihuahua is popular around the world for his spirited, intelligent, and loving personality. The AKC breed standard refers to his ineffable expression as "saucy," an adjective that Merriam-Webster defines as "impertinently bold and impudent" and "amusingly forward and flippant." In other words, the Chihuahua is confident like no other dog. Despite his six pounds (or less), he will

stand up to any dog, no matter the height or weight, completely unaware of his diminutive stature.

In fact, adult Chihuahuas can weigh as little as one pound, making the Chihuahua the smallest breed in the world. The AKC standard states "weight not to exceed 6 pounds," while European standards say that weight can be between 500 grams and 3 kilograms (1–6 pounds), with a preference for 1–2 kilograms (2–4 pounds). In both Europe and America, dogs weighing over 3 kilograms (6 pounds) are disqualified from competition in the show ring.

Chihuahuas come in two coat varieties, long and smooth. Long-coated Chihuahuas have soft, flat, or slightly wavy hair with excess feathering on the ears, tail, and legs. Smooth-coated Chihuahuas have glossy, short, straight hair. And both long and smooth Chihuahuas come in almost every color.

PEOPLE OF THE CHI

Were you born to be a Chihuahuan? The only thing small about the Chihuahua is his size—not his personality, attitude, ego, or heart. He's an active little dog with a big story to tell. He is tremendously loyal and always wants to be close to his owner. Your life won't be your own anymore, and there will be little privacy!

Chihuahuas never fully outgrow their puppy mischief, often tearing up magazines, digging up flowers, and chasing the family cat well into their adult years. The breed's saucy personality and unquenchable curiosity will provide years of amusement for its keepers. Most owners accept the Chi's inventive naughtiness and welcome their games and clowning. Chihuahuas are often compared to a small terrier for their feisty tendencies and their enjoyment of digging. Also like

terriers, Chihuahuas have big opinions and don't hesitate to share them. If you live in close proximity to your neighbors, they may not appreciate your barky pooch. Extra training and socialization can keep the Chihuahua's vociferous inclinations in check.

SMALL PACKAGES

Owners find the Chihuahua's diminutive size enormously convenient. If you travel frequently, he can easily fit into a pet carrier or your carry-on bag—just make sure to check the airline's policies on traveling with animals. The Chi is an ideal travel companion, never hogging the arm rests or your complimentary peanuts! Undeniably one of the breed's most alluring traits is its portability, but the Chihuahua is anything but an attractive accessory. If this is your main reason for wanting a Chihuahua, you'd be wiser to buy a silk scarf or a designer handbag.

While the Chihuahua doesn't mind the soft interior of a luxurious Fendi bag, toting your Chi around town with you encourages strangers to reach out unexpectedly and pet your dog. Make sure that you thoroughly socialize your Chihuahua so that this does not scare him or lead to a fear of strangers. Most Chihuahuas will quickly get comfortable in your handbag and doze off for an hour or two. But his siesta won't last forever! Be aware that a bored Chihuahua may simply hop out of the bag whenever he likes. Leaping from your bag to the floor could be a fatal fall, like jumping off the roof of a two-story house. Never leave your Chihuahua unattended when your bag is open or sitting in a high place.

Chihuahuas enjoy and need exercise and outdoor play as much as any other breed. Take your Chi for a short walk every day to keep him physically and mentally in shape.

The Chihuahua's fear is as diminutive as he is. It is safer (and healthier!) for your Chihuahua to walk at your side on a leash. He'll get more exercise and be able to explore the world more fully by using all of his canine senses.

ONE, TWO, MAYBE THREE?

Chihuahua owners enjoy taking their dogs for walks around the neighborhood. In fact, experienced Chihuahua fanciers say it's just as easy to walk two or three Chihuahuas as it is to walk one. A brisk walk (always on leash, of course) around your neighborhood, a ten-minute break in the backyard, or even an indoor romp around your living room or down your hallway will suffice for the Chihuahua's daily exercise regimen. Most important to the Chihuahua is that you spend quality playtime with him, inside or out.

Doting dog-lovers who live alone make great Chihuahua parents. The playful Chi will return the love and dedication of his devoted owners tenfold. Some owners even say that Chihuahuas are not dogs at all—they're four-legged babies! Now, what more cherished baby could you possibly have?

SUMMER LOVIN'

Chihuahuas are derived from the warm climate of Mexico, where summer temperatures can easily climb over 100 degrees Fahrenheit. Sun-worshipers adore the Chihuahua, who will happily laze in the afternoon sun for hours alongside you. On less sunny days, your Chi will seek out even the tiniest ray to take his siesta beneath. But take care that neither of you gets overheated nor sunburned! Even though the breed is from a desert region, any dog can get heatstroke.

On the other hand, winter is not the Chihuahua's favorite season. The breed can easily lose body heat, so invest in a doggy sweater for the cooler months. In very cold weather, your Chi (long- or smooth-coated) may not even want to venture outside.

A WORD OF CAUTION

Owners of the world's smallest dog have the biggest responsibilities keeping their Chihuahuas safe and out of harm's way. Because they're fearless and unknowingly reckless, Chihuahuas will jump from heights many times their own. Owners must be mindful whenever their high-flying dogs are on tabletops, chairs, beds, and so forth. Broken legs and head injuries are not uncommon; and remember that the Chihuahua's skull is very fragile, especially as a young dog.

Chihuahuas are decidedly familial, meaning they like to hang out with their own kind. They may not do well with larger dogs that can unintentionally hurt them while playing or roughhousing. The Chi's bravery can also get the breed into fights with larger dogs (which is pretty much all other dogs) and cats, too. Owners have to be protective of their dogs for their safety.

Likewise, owners must be cautious when walking their Chis so that their pets aren't mistaken as prey by other dogs. Never allow your Chihuahua off leash when on a walk or even when spending time on your own front lawn. Chihuahuas run fast, but not fast enough. A Greyhound or Whippet running toward your Chihuahua may not recognize him as another dog, but rather may mistake him for a rabbit or a cat.

Also be wary of two-footed predators, aka children! Boisterous kids who are unfamiliar with dogs or who have larger dogs of their own can easily injure the small Chihuahua. Young children can grab at a Chi or accidentally drop him, so supervision is always mandatory.

What's in a Name!

The name Chihuahua derives from an Uto-Aztecan word, either Nahuatl or Tarahumaran, meaning, "between two waters" or "place where rivers meet," namely the Rio Grande and the Conchos River. There are thirty Native American languages in the Uto-Aztecan family and many of them are still spoken today.

Protect your Chihuahua from curious children, rambunctious dogs, and most importantly, himself! Chihuahuas often see themselves as larger-than-life, and they won't hesitate to leap into harm's way.

Responsible Pet Ownership

AMERICAN
KENNEL CLUB®

Getting a dog is exciting, but it's also a huge responsibility. That's why it's important to educate yourself on all that is involved in being a good pet owner. As a part of the Canine Good Citizen® test, the AKC has a "Responsible Dog Owner's Pledge," which states:

I will be responsible for my dog's health needs.

☐ I will provide routine veterinary care, including check-ups and vaccines.

☐ I will offer adequate nutrition through proper diet and clean water at all times.

☐ I will give daily exercise and regularly bathe and groom.

I will be responsible for my dog's safety.

☐ I will properly control my dog by providing fencing where appropriate, by not letting my dog run loose, and by using a leash in public.

☐ I will ensure that my dog has some form of identification when appropriate (which may include collar tags, tattoos, or microchip identification).

☐ I will provide adequate supervision when my dog and children are together.

I will not allow my dog to infringe on the rights of others.

☐ I will not allow my dog to run loose in the neighborhood.

☐ I will not allow my dog to be a nuisance to others by barking while in the yard, in a hotel room, etc.

☐ I will pick up and properly dispose of my dog's waste in all public areas, such as on the grounds of hotels, on sidewalks, in parks, etc.

☐ I will pick up and properly dispose of my dog's waste in wilderness areas, on hiking trails, on campgrounds, and in off-leash parks.

I will be responsible for my dog's quality of life.

☐ I understand that basic training is beneficial to all dogs.

☐ I will give my dog attention and playtime.

☐ I understand that owning a dog is a commitment in time and caring.

A BIG HEART

What outweighs all of the Chihuahua's naughtiness and haughtiness is a quality that no breeder or lover of the Chihuahua would deny: unabashed sweetness. He is a very sweet little dog, and his heart is many times his size. The Chihuahua loves his owner completely, and his eyes say so. They glisten with tenderness and a genuine quality that no other dog possesses. Chihuahuas love big: his love for you knows no bounds, and he expects you to love him even more in return.

The Chihuahua comes in two coat types—smooth and long. Long-coated Chis require a little more grooming time, but because of the breed's tiny size, coat care takes just a few minutes daily.

At a Glance ...

The warm, loving eyes of a Chihuahua will melt your heart. Though the breed is the smallest in the world, the Chihuahua's personality is anything but tiny. Chihuahuas are treasured for their larger-than-life personas and unending devotion to their owners.

Chihuahuas are small, dainty dogs with big superman complexes. As such, you'll need to keep a close eye on your Chihuahua to make sure that he doesn't try to jump from heights—or pick fights with other dogs—more than twice his size.

Due to the breed's small size and devoted personalities, it's hard not to want more than one Chihuahua! Luckily, the breed thrives in multi-Chi households. Consider your own lifestyle and habits before purchasing a second (or third!) Chihuahua. Make sure that you have the time and finances necessary to dedicate to each and every one of your canine kids.

CHAPTER TWO

Chihuahua Essentials

A popular member of the Toy Group, the Chihuahua has been highly regarded as a companion for centuries. Its direct ancestor, the Techichi, was a small, heavy-boned dog breed that served as a popular companion in early Central America, dating back to the 9th century AD. The compact, graceful modern Chihuahua, coated in a smooth, soft, glossy coat or a long, slightly wavy coat, continues to win hearts in homes and show rings around the world.

The modern Chihuahua is quite different from its ancient Central American ancestor, the Techichi. Today's Chis are more petite, with larger ears and shorter muzzles.

The official breed standard, written by the Chihuahua Club of America, the breed's parent club, and approved by the American Kennel Club, describes the ideal Chihuahua, detailing physical traits, character, and movement. It is this standard that judges use in the show ring and breeders use as they plan their litters. Chihuahuas that win in the show ring have a veritable "stamp of approval" from judges that they are worthy of breeding future generations.

THE IDEAL CHIHUAHUA

Let's take a look at the characteristics of the ideal Chihuahua. The head of the Chihuahua is regarded as its most distinguishing feature. Its skull is "apple-domed," its cheeks and jaws lean, and its muzzle fairly short and pointed. There may or may not be a molera, a cranial gap in the skull that has not closed with

A PIECE OF HISTORY

The American Kennel Club's stud book makes reference to four unregistered Chihuahuas in 1890 named Anno, Bob, Eyah, and Pepity. Those four are followed by Chihuahueria and Nita, recorded in 1894. The Chihuahua breed was officially recognized by the AKC in 1904, and the first dog registered was a long coat aptly named Midget!

maturity. The dog's large round eyes do not protrude, and they are set well apart, their center on a line with the lowest point of the large, flaring ears and the base of the muzzle, which joins with the head in a definite stop. Eyes can vary in color, as can pigment, according to the color of the dog.

The head is set on a slightly arched, medium-length neck, sloping gracefully into laid-back and lean shoulders. The topline is level, the ribs well sprung but not barreled, and the lower chest deep. The Chihuahua is slightly longer from his shoulder to the buttocks than he is in height at the withers (shoulders), with somewhat shorter bodies seen on males.

Although this is a tiny and dainty breed, the Chihuahua has muscular hindquarters, giving drive from behind and helping the dog to move with brisk, forceful action. A high-stepping or hackney action, as seen in the Italian Greyhound, is not characteristic. The feet should turn neither in nor out, and, when viewed on the move, the legs should be neither too wide nor too close. Forelegs are flexible and the feet small and dainty; the toes are well divided but not spread.

The tail of the Chihuahua is rather special. It is of medium length, set high and carried up and over the back in sickle fashion. The Chihuahua breed standard states that the tail is "carried sickle either up or out, or in a loop over the back, with tip just touching the back." Ideally it is flat, broadening slightly in the center and tapering to a point.

There are two coat types. The smooth variety has a soft-textured coat that is close and glossy. An undercoat and ruff are permissible in smooths. Preferably,

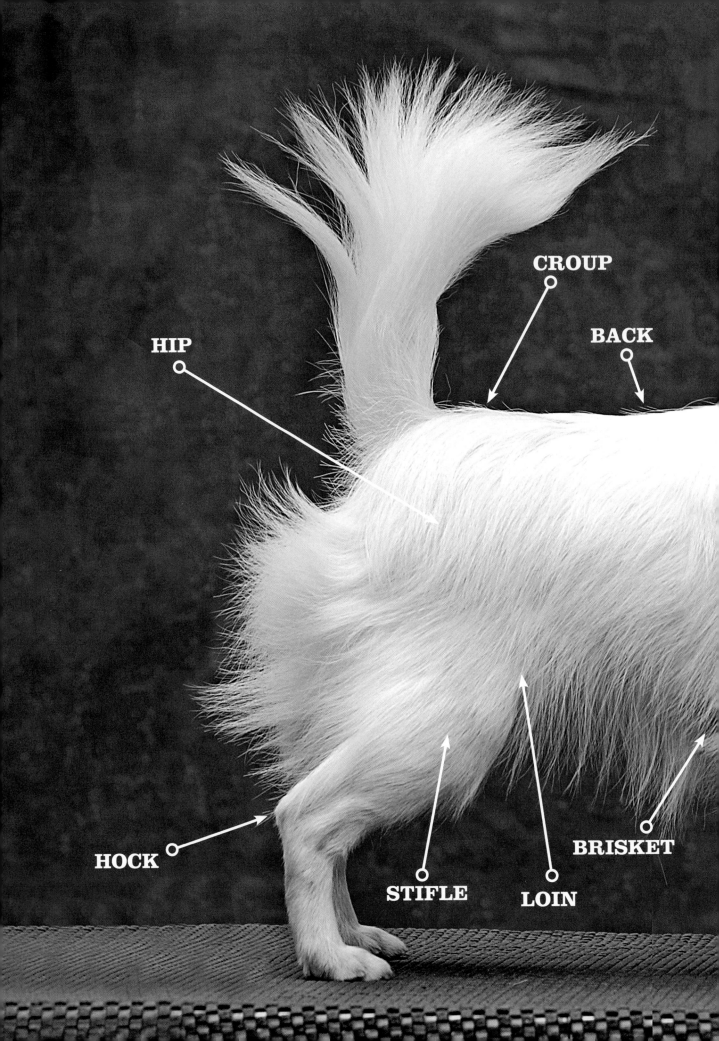

CROUP

BACK

HIP

HOCK

STIFLE

LOIN

BRISKET

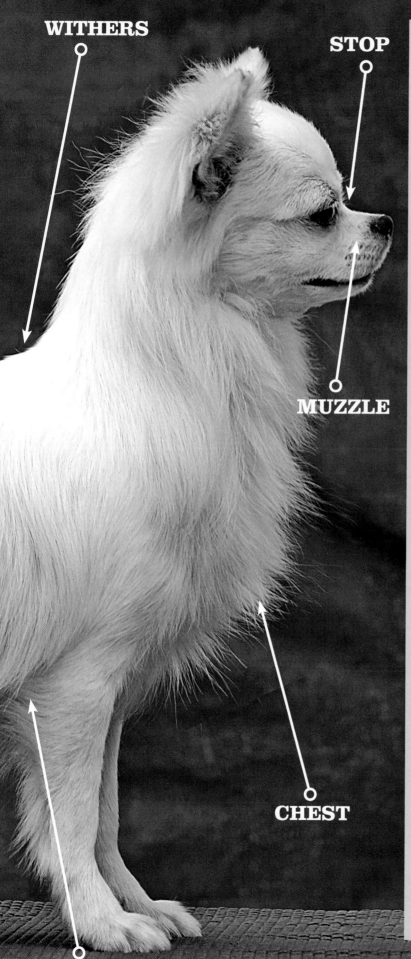

WITHERS

STOP

MUZZLE

CHEST

ELBOW

The Chihuahua in Brief

COUNTRY OF ORIGIN:
Mexico

ORIGINAL USE:
Companionship

GROUP:
Toy

AVERAGE LIFE SPAN:
13 to 17 years

COAT:
Two varieties: long coat has a soft texture and is either flat or silky and wavy; smooth coat is soft, close, and glossy.

COLOR:
Any color or combination of colors with markings, splashing, merling, or masks.

GROOMING:
The long coat requires gentle brushing daily; the smooth coat requires little grooming, a weekly once-over with a soft-bristle brush suffices.

WEIGHT:
1 to 6 pounds

TRAINABILITY:
Moderate to high

PERSONALITY:
Full of himself, assured, bold, and feisty; unaware of his mere inches; his saucy expression speaks volumes about his fearless attitude.

ACTIVITY LEVEL:
Moderate to high

GOOD WITH OTHER PETS:
Chihuahuas prefer to share their home with humans and other Chihuahuas.

NATIONAL BREED CLUB:
Chihuahua Club of America; www.chihuahuaclubofamerica.com

RESCUE:
Chihuahua Club of America; www.chihuahuaclubofamerica.com/breed-info/rescue

The Chihuahua comes in just about every color and pattern. Choose a Chi based on his structure and personality; color is simply a matter of preference.

Meet the Parent Club

The Chihuahua Club of America is the national parent club for the breed, and a member of the American Kennel Club. The club was established in 1923, nineteen years after the Chihuahua was recognized by the AKC and eleven years before the breed was recognized in Mexico, the breed's country of origin. The mission of the parent club is "to encourage and promote quality in breeding of pure-bred Chihuahuas and if at all possible to bring their natural qualities to perfection." For more information, visit the club's website at www.chihuahuaclubofamerica.com.

the hair on the tail should be furry. Long-coated Chihuahuas also have a soft-textured coat, which can be either flat or slightly wavy. The coat should never be tight and curly, coarse, or harsh to the touch. There is feathering on the ears, feet, and legs, and there are "pants" on the hindquarters. A large ruff on the neck is desirable, and the tail is long and full, forming a plume. Both coat varieties possess a soft and dense undercoat; smooths may have a heavier undercoat.

The Chihuahua is nearly limitless in color, from white to black, with various markings, splashing, or plain solid. The Chihuahua Club of America identifies the following colors: black, chocolate, cream, fawn, red, black, blue, gold, silver, and white, possibly combined with tan, white, cream, or red markings or with brindling (a dark pattern over a sandy or gray background), sabling (a dark brown that is almost black), merle (a bluish or reddish gray mixed with splotches of black), and blue or black masks.

MARCH OF THE TOYS

The Chihuahua is a member of the AKC Toy Group, an elite squad of tiny pure-bred companion dogs. The Chihuahua is, of course, the smallest dog in the group, and the Cavalier King Charles Spaniel is the largest. All Toy dogs exist to bring their owners joy, delight, and companionship, and the Chihuahua excels at all of these things naturally. The Chi's self-assured personality and his macho carriage can't fail to entertain his spellbound owners. The Toy Group is well armed with

Long-coated Chihuahua's ears, tail, legs, and chest should be combed daily to prevent tangles and to keep the hair soft and silky.

The Chihuahua Breed Standard

AMERICAN KENNEL CLUB

GENERAL APPEARANCE: A graceful, alert, swift-moving compact little dog with saucy expression, and with terrier-like qualities of temperament.

SIZE, PROPORTION, SUBSTANCE

Weight—A well balanced little dog not to exceed 6 pounds. *Proportion*—The body is off-square; hence, slightly longer when measured from point of shoulder to point of buttocks, than height at the withers. Somewhat shorter bodies are preferred in males. *Disqualification*—Any dog over 6 pounds in weight.

HEAD

A well-rounded "apple dome" skull, with or without molera. *Expression*—Saucy. *Eyes*—Full, round, but not protruding, balanced, set well apart; luminous dark or luminous ruby. *Ears*—Large, erect type ears, held more upright when alert, but flaring to the sides at a 45 degree angle when in repose, giving breadth between the ears. *Stop*—Well defined. *Muzzle*—Moderately short, slightly pointed. *Nose*—Self-colored or black. *Bite*—Level or scissors. *Disqualifications*—Broken down or cropped ears.

NECKLINE, TOPLINE, BODY

Neck—Slightly arched, gracefully sloping into lean shoulders. *Topline*—Level. *Body*—Ribs rounded and well sprung (but not too much "barrel-shaped"). *Tail*—Moderately long, carried sickle either up or out, or in a loop over the back with tip just touching the back. *Disqualifications*—Docked tail, bobtail.

FOREQUARTERS

Shoulders—Lean, sloping into a slightly broadening support above straight forelegs that set well under, giving free movement at the elbows. *Feet*—A small, dainty foot with toes well split up but not spread, pads cushioned. *Pasterns*—Strong.

HINDQUARTERS

Muscular, with hocks well apart, neither out nor in, well let down, firm and sturdy.

COAT

In the Smooth Coats, the coat should be of soft texture, close and glossy. (Heavier coats with undercoats permissible.) Coat placed well over body with ruff on neck preferred, and more scanty on head and ears. Hair on tail preferred furry. In Long Coats, the coat should be of a soft texture, either flat or slightly wavy, with undercoat preferred. *Ears*—Fringed. *Tail*—Full and long (as a plume). Feathering on feet and legs, pants on hind legs and large ruff on the neck desired and preferred. *Disqualification*—In Long Coats, too thin coat that resembles bareness.

COLOR

Any color—solid, marked, or splashed.

GAIT

The Chihuahua should move swiftly with a firm, sturdy action, with good reach in front equal to the drive from the rear. The topline should remain firm and the backline level as the dog moves.

TEMPERAMENT

Alert, projecting the "terrier-like" attitudes of self importance, confidence, self-reliance.

—Excerpts from the American Kennel Club Breed Standard

alarm dogs, alert and territorial little watchdogs that don't hesitate to sound an alarm when danger is perceived. Because the average Chihuahua sees himself as the size of a German Shepherd, his bark is impressive and is definitely worse than his bite. This feisty nature ties into what the breed standard refers to as "terrier-like qualities of temperament." Chihuahuas can be stubborn and determined, like terriers, and may even chase a mouse or dig a hole when the mood strikes them.

CAN'T GET ENOUGH?

Learn even more about the Chihuahua on the American Kennel Club website, www.akc.org, or visit the Chihuahua Club of America website, www.chihuahuaclubofamerica.com. After everything you've read and researched, if you still feel that the Chihuahua is the perfect fit for your household, the next step is to meet with a few Chihuahua owners and breeders to get the inside scoop on this lovable, tiny breed. Through the Chihuahua Club of America, you can find your local Chihuahua breed club. The breed club will get you in touch with Chihuahua owners so that you can meet and talk with them firsthand about their experiences as devoted Chihuahua lovers. Don't hesitate to ask questions! Deciding to add a Chihuahua—or any dog for that matter—to your life is a big decision, and you want to be well informed as you take the leap into dog ownership.

At a Glance ...

The Toy Group is made up of twenty-one tiny dogs known for their enthusiasm, devotion, and companionship. Weighing in at 6 pounds or less, the Chihuahua is the smallest dog in the Group, but don't let his diminutive size fool you: his big, outgoing personality more than makes up for his tiny stature.

The Chihuahua is a dog of many colors. All coat colors in both long- and smooth-coated dogs are permissible, including black, chocolate, cream, fawn, red, black, blue, gold, silver, and white, possibly combined with tan, white, cream, or red markings, or with brindling, sabling, merle, and blue or black masks...to name just a few.

Visit the American Kennel Club website, www.akc.org, and the Chihuahua Club of America website, www.chihuahuaclubofamerica.com, to learn more about this small but confident breed. Choosing the right dog for your lifestyle is a big decision, so learn all you can about the needs and personality of this breed before you start looking for breeders.

CHAPTER THREE

A Chi of Your Very Own

The beginning of a Chihuahua puppy search can be both overwhelming and exciting. Due to the breed's popularity, there are many Chihuahua breeders to choose from, and your job is to locate one who is responsible and dedicated to the breed. Prospective puppy buyers should always keep foremost in their minds that there are many different kinds of breeders, some with the breed's best interest at heart, and others with only profit on the mind. Chihuahuas

A Teacup or Tiny Toy?

According to the Chihuahua Club of America, a Chihuahua is a Chihuahua is a Chihuahua! The breed comes in two coat varieties, long and smooth. Even though the weight range in the breed standard, from 1 to 6 pounds, is fairly broad, a 1-pound Chihuahua is unusually small and not a special variety. Avoid breeders who attempt to label their Chis as "Teacup," "Tiny Toy," "Pocket Size," "Mini," and so forth. Small Chihuahuas aren't rare, exceptional, or any more valuable than any other healthy, sound Chihuahua. Unusually small Chihuahuas can be perfectly healthy but, due to their extreme petiteness, they do require extra care, and buyers should be cautioned before acquiring the tiniest of the tiny.

are small dogs that are inexpensive to feed and require very little space—many disreputable, profit-seeking breeders take advantage of the breed's minimal requirements. It is essential that you locate a breeder who not only has attractive dogs you admire but also does proper health screening for all of his or her stock. A healthy, sound Chi can live well into his teenage years—what's your hurry? If you have to wait for a puppy from the breeder of your choice, then wait. The time spent will be worth it, and you'll be grateful for many years to come.

THE RIGHT BREEDER

Fortunately for Chihuahua lovers, there are many good breeders around, and if you look carefully, you will find one. The AKC (www.akc.org) and the Chihuahua Club of America (www.chihuahuaclubofamerica.com) are sources you can trust to provide contact information of reputable breeders in your area. Breeders listed as AKC Breeders of Merit program participants are great choices to begin your search. No matter where you find a breeder, you still need to meet the breeder to be sure that his or her standards of breeding and care are what you expect. You must be sure that the breeder has taken into consideration the health, soundness, and pedigrees of his or her breeding stock.

You don't need to buy a book to learn that the Chihuahua is a small dog—a very small dog. Just as in people, size can vary from dog to dog. That's not to say that you should be looking for a 15-pound Chihuahua, but you shouldn't be looking for a ½-pound Chihuahua either! Good breeders produce healthy Chihuahuas that are correctly sized, and they won't mislead customers by claiming they are selling anything rare or exotic.

Whether weighing 1 pound or 6 pounds, the Chihuahua—without exception—is an inside dog. The breeder you select should be someone who has raised the puppies in his or her own home. It is unlikely to find a reputable Chihuahua breeder who is housing all of his or her dogs in a kennel environment. Small dogs don't do well in such an environment.

THE RIGHT PUPPY

Regardless of how large or small the breeder's program, all of the Chihuahua puppies should be clean and well looked after, and living in a sanitary, suitable environment. All of the puppies should be in tip-top condition and be happy, confident, and friendly.

A Chihuahua puppy should strike you as vital, alert, and healthy, without any sign of discharge from his eyes or nose. The puppy's body should feel firm and solid. His rear end should be spotless, with no sign of redness or diarrhea. Although a puppy's nails can be sharp, they should be neatly trimmed and not overly long. The skin should look healthy and the coat should be in excellent condition: not tacky, flaky, or sparse in any way, and with no sign of parasites. Fleas and lice cannot always be seen easily, but an itchy puppy gives you a big hint, and you might notice a rash. Keep in mind, however, that scratching does not always mean that the puppy has a parasitic or skin condition, for it can also be associated with teething. In this case, the puppy will only scratch around his head area due to the discomfort in his mouth. This will stop around seven or eight months of age when the Chihuahua's second set of teeth comes through and his gums are no longer sore.

Observe how the puppies move. Compare the puppies' body structure to the many Chihuahuas you see in this book or that you may have seen at dog shows. The puppies should be able to move around freely without hindrance. If any puppies seem to be reluctant to move around, ask the breeder why.

A litter of Chihuahuas should be a feast for your eyes as well as your nose. Puppies should not be stinky. The ears should be clean and odorless, and the puppies themselves should smell dry and fresh.

You have a few important decisions to make when choosing a Chihuahua. The Chihuahua is bred in two different coat types: long and smooth. The smooth-coated Chihuahua is more recognizable, having appeared in many movies and commercials. The smooth coat is soft and glossy and easy to care for, but an owner must take into account protecting the smooth-coated Chihuahua in

Get Your Registration and Pedigree

A responsible breeder will be able to provide your family with an American Kennel Club registration form and pedigree.

AKC REGISTRATION: When you buy a Chihuahua from a breeder, ask the breeder for an American Kennel Club Dog Registration Application form. The breeder will fill out most of the application for you. When you fill out your portion of the document and mail it to the AKC, you will receive a Registration Certificate proving that your dog is officially part of the AKC. Besides recording your name and your dog's name in the AKC database, registration helps fund the AKC's good works such as canine health research, search-and-rescue teams, educating the public about responsible dog care, and much more.

CERTIFIED PEDIGREE: A pedigree is an AKC certificate proving that your dog is a purebred. It shows your puppy's family tree, listing the names of his parents and grandparents. If your dog is registered with the AKC, the organization will have a copy of your dog's pedigree on file, which you can order from its website (www.akc.org). Look for any titles that your Chihuahua's ancestors have won, including Champion (conformation), Companion Dog (obedience), and so forth. A pedigree doesn't guarantee the health or personality of a dog, but it's a starting point for picking out a good Chihuahua puppy.

inclement weather. The long-coated Chihuahua is a bit more unique, with a slightly wavy texture, undercoat, and feathering along the ears, chest, and tail. The long coat requires basic daily brushing and grooming, a slightly more time-consuming task than is required for smooth-coat care.

There is also the decision of whether to choose a male or a female Chihuahua. Essentially, male and female Chihuahuas are the same in both stature and personality, with just a few differences to keep in mind. A male Chihuahua can be more territorial than a female, that is, more protective of his home and his people, and have the urge to roam. A female Chihuahua, on the other hand, has the tendency to be moody if she is in heat. If neutered or spayed, male and female Chihuahuas usually lose these sex-based personality traits—or they are dampened significantly. Regardless of whether you choose a male or a female, it's most important to find a healthy and sound puppy with an outgoing, upbeat personality.

Many breeders allow prospective buyers to view the puppies at about five or six weeks, but due to their small size, Chihuahuas usually don't move to their new homes until around ten to twelve weeks of age. Though devoted to their owners, Chis can often be suspicious of those they don't know, so early socialization is paramount. By five or six weeks of age, most puppies are outgoing and looking for some fast fun. Look for a pup that clearly enjoys the attention of people. When you go to select your puppy, take along the other members of your family. Every member of your household should be on board with the important decision of bringing a "four-legged baby" into your home. A Chihuahua will most likely change all of your lives.

No matter their size, Chihuahua puppies should be happy, outgoing, and eager to meet new people. Your breeder should already have begun socializing his or her Chis before you meet them for the first time.

MEET THE PARENTS

Look forward to meeting the dam (mother) of the litter. The breeder should be proud to introduce you to his or her adult dogs, especially the mother of the puppies you're admiring. She may look a little tired from taking care of her demanding puppies, but she should still be friendly to visitors. Many dams are protective of their litters, so it may take a little while for her to size you up. Observe how the dam interacts with her offspring. A mom with a sound temperament will be affectionate and tolerant with her pups. If the dam is not available for you to see, this may be a red flag. The absence of the dam might be an indication that the puppies were not born on the premises, but have been brought in from elsewhere to be sold. It's very unlikely that the breeder would allow the dam to be "off at the shows" or "visiting a friend." This might be your cue to move on to the next breeder.

If the sire (father) of the litter is not available, that is more common, for he may well be owned by another breeder. Some breeders travel hundreds of miles to use the services of a desirable sire, and artificial insemination is common among show breeders. Nonetheless, dedicated breeders will at least be able to show you the sire's photo and pedigree, as well as tell you about him.

QUESTIONS FROM BREEDERS

Responsible breeders are some of the most inquisitive folk on the planet, or so it will seem when you first contact them. Don't be intimidated or put off by the breeder's line of questioning: it indicates that he or she cares about the puppies and wants to see that each one goes to the best possible home. If the breeder has no questions for you other than "Will you be paying with cash or credit?" then you should be worried.

Here are a few common questions that responsible breeders ask prospective puppy buyers:

• **Is this your first dog?** Breeders want to know how much experience you have with dogs in general. Dog care and training is more complicated than raising goldfish or growing orchids, so the more firsthand experience you have with dogs, the better. If you grew up with a dog, be sure you tell the breeder all about it. Breeders are never impressed by curt, nonchalant answers: they're looking for potential dog owners who will love and fawn over their puppies.

• **Are there children in the household?** The age of your children will be a concern for Chihuahua breeders. They want to be sure that the kids are old enough to safely handle the puppy to avoid any injuries to the dog.

Why Should You Register with the American Kennel Club?

Registering your puppy with the American Kennel Club helps the AKC do many good things for dogs everywhere, such as promote responsible breeding and support the care and health of dogs throughout the country. As a result of your registration, the AKC is able to inspect kennels across the country, educate dog owners about the importance of training through the Canine Good Citizen® Program, support search-and-rescue canines via the AKC Companion Animal Recovery Canine Support and Relief Fund, teach the public about the importance of responsible dog ownership through publications and the annual AKC Responsible Dog Ownership Days, and much more. Not only is the AKC a respected organization dedicated to the registration of purebred dogs, but it is also devoted to the well-being of dogs everywhere. For more information, visit the AKC registration webpage at www.akc.org/reg.

Ranging from 1 to 6 pounds, all Chihuahuas are small, but don't seek out breeders that advertise smaller-than-normal puppies. These profit-minded breeders are more interested in money than the well-being of their litters.

• **What kind of dog-training experience do you have?** Every dog needs training, regardless of his size or temperament. Without training and socialization, Toy dogs can be just as difficult to manage as large dogs. Chihuahuas are naturally bright animals and can be trained to do many things, including compete in agility and obedience trials. The breeder will love to hear that you're interested in enrolling in a local training class and maybe even taking the AKC Canine Good Citizen test. If you'd like to show your puppy or register him as a therapy dog, be sure to share your hopes and intentions with the breeder so that he or she can help you choose the right puppy.

• **Do you have a yard with a fence?** Unleashed Chihuahuas can never be allowed outside unless safely confined within a yard or fenced-in area.

• **Do you work full-time?** Chihuahuas do not fend well for themselves when left alone all day. If you and the other adults in the household work all day, then it is best to find day-care assistance for your dog. Making arrangements with a professional dog walker or dog sitter will show the breeder that you're serious about looking after the puppy. You may also be able to ask a neighbor or family friend to visit the house regularly to check on the dog and to let him outside for a bathroom and play break. Any situation is better than leaving the Chihuahua alone for hours on end.

QUESTIONS FOR BREEDERS

Your breeder shouldn't be the only one asking questions. Here are a few common questions to ask your breeder when looking for the right puppy:

• **How long have you been breeding Chihuahuas?** The longer the breeder has been involved in breeding and showing Chihuahuas, the better. It's never encouraging to hear that this is the breeder's first or second litter, though it's not necessarily a deal breaker either.

• **Are you involved with the Chihuahua Club of America, and do you show your own dogs?** Find out how active the breeder is with the national breed club. It's a good sign if the breeder is in good standing with the parent club. Even if you're not interested in showing your dog, this is a good question. Dog shows are the accepted forum to determine the best breeding animals. Participating in dog shows demonstrates the breeder's interest in testing his or her breeding stock by getting judges' opinions of the dogs.

• **Have you bred many Champions? Are you an AKC Breeder of Merit program participant?** Most breeders are extremely proud of the number of champions they've produced and will not be modest about sharing the statistics. The AKC Breeder of Merit program, which the American Kennel Club describes as "the heart of the AKC," honors conscientious breeders who have at least five years' involvement with the AKC, have earned at least four titles on dogs they bred or co-bred, and who certify health screening and guarantee all puppies are registered with the AKC.

• **Do you guarantee the puppy's health?** The breeder's sales contract may offer a money-back guarantee if the puppy develops a health disorder within the first year or two of his life. A responsible breeder will promise to accept the puppy back at any time if things do not work out.

• **Can you provide references of other owners of your puppies?** Naturally, breeders will only give you names of people who they believe are happy with their puppies. Check with them anyway. Not everyone shares every detail of the puppy's health and temperament with the breeder. Also ask the breeder to provide the name and contact information for his or her veterinarian so that you can contact him or her about the health of the breeder's litters.

• **At what age do you release puppies?** Most breeders will not release Chihuahua puppies until they are at least ten weeks of age, possibly even twelve or fourteen weeks, due to their small size. If you find a breeder who is willing to release a five- or six-week-old puppy to you, it's likely not a puppy you want.

Can't decide on a smooth- or long-coated Chi? While long coats require daily brushing to keep their fur fresh and clean, smooth coats may need extra protection from cold climates such as dog sweaters or jackets.

WHAT TO EXPECT

Once you've chosen the right Chihuahua, your breeder will pull out a large packet of materials for you concerning your new puppy. Be sure that this packet includes a sales contract, pedigree and registration papers, the puppy's health certifications and vaccination history (as well as the health certifications of his mother and father), and feeding instructions for you to follow to make your puppy's transition to his new home as easy as possible.

An official sales contract between you and the breeder is a must. The contract should outline the puppy's cost, health guarantees, and reasonable return policies. It may also include a spay/neuter requirement if you will not be showing your dog.

The breeder should have already registered the litter with the American Kennel Club, and he or she will provide you with a partially filled out AKC Dog Registration Application for you to finish and mail to the AKC or submit online at www.akc.org. Within a few weeks, you will receive an AKC Registration Certificate for your puppy. Your breeder should also provide a pedigree for your puppy, detailing your Chihuahua's family tree going back at least three generations. This shows your puppy's purebred heritage and will tell you if he has any champions in his bloodline.

The puppies in the litter should have already been examined by a veterinarian, who will provide the breeder with a health certificate that includes which vaccinations and wormings the puppies have received. The breeder will also provide any other relevant health screening documentation to you at the time of purchase. Visit the Chihuahua Club of America's website to find out what health tests the club recommends for breeders. Don't hesitate to ask the breeder to see written proof of the test dates and results. Most breeders provide a health guarantee for the puppy with a "no-questions-asked" return policy. Trusted breeders care about the happiness and well-being of their puppies, and should be willing to take the puppy back at any time in his life if things don't work out.

Breeders will most likely ask you a lot of questions. Don't be put off by the interrogation. The more questions breeders ask, the more you know that they care about the happiness of their puppies.

CHOOSE WISELY

The key to finding the right breeder is to ask lots of questions. Your breeder should be happy to answer any and all questions you

have, no matter how simple they may be. A well-chosen breeder will be able to give a new puppy owner much useful guidance, including tips about feeding, handling, crate-training, and so forth. The best breeders will act as a reference and go-to source for advice throughout your Chihuahua's life. Choose your breeder carefully, and you will be rewarded with a healthy, happy Chihuahua for life.

At a Glance ...

Take the time to find the right breeder. Patience when choosing a puppy will be rewarded with years of health and happiness in the years to come. Contact the Chihuahua Club of America (www .chihuahuaclubofamerica.com) or your local breed club to find a responsible breeder near you.

A reputable breeder will not hesitate to show you paperwork documenting the health of his or her dogs—both puppies and parents. Never take a breeder at his or her word alone; get copies of everything in writing. At the very least, this includes a puppy sales contract, pedigree and registration papers, and health records and documentation.

All puppies are cute, and the tiny Chihuahua is no exception. Don't fall for the first pair of glistening Chi eyes you see. Be sure that the litter you choose is healthy, outgoing, and friendly—how a dog behaves in the first months of life should indicate what he will be like as an adult.

CHAPTER FOUR

A Chihuahua in the House

Before you bring your Chihuahua puppy home for the first time, you have lots of planning to do. A puppy, no matter how tiny, will turn your home life upside down. The better you plan for his arrival, the smoother and more enjoyable the first days will be for you and your pup. There are lots of decisions to make—where he will sleep, eat, play, and relieve himself—before you carry your Chihuahua through the front door.

Your Chihuahua will need plenty of toys to keep him mentally stimulated. Choose just a few toys at first to determine which types your Chi will favor.

His sleeping area, where you'll place his bed and/or crate, must be in a comfortable, safe, warm place, well away from drafts. If you have a backyard, you must be certain that it's absolutely secure. Tiny Chihuahua puppies can simply walk through your chain-link fence (if the links are too wide), so be sure to reinforce the lower part of the fence. There's also a bit of shopping ahead of you to purchase the basic accessories you'll need for your puppy, including bowls, leashes, collars, toys, grooming supplies, and, of course, his own special puppy food.

A PIECE OF HISTORY

Though the Chihuahua has been kept as a pet in Britain since the 1850s, the breed did not become popular in the United States until the early 1900s. The tiny breed was already a common choice as a lady's companion, but the rise of the Chihuahua in US popular culture grew as celebrities such as Lupe Velez, Lauren Bacall, and Xavier Cugat were publicly seen with their own pet Chis in the 1930s and 1940s. In the decades following World War II, the Chihuahua suddenly rocketed to the third most popular breed in the Toy Group. Even today, the Chihuahua is a popular choice among celebrities such as Paris Hilton, Britney Spears, Elijah Wood, and Madonna.

SHOP 'TIL YOU DROP

Before your Chihuahua arrives, discuss the puppy's needs with the breeder. He or she will give you guidance about what kind of collar, leash, food, bowls, brushes, and so forth to buy. Relying on an experienced Chihuahua person's firsthand knowledge is better than any advice you'll find online or at the pet-supply store to ensure that your pup's first days and weeks in your home are safe, fun, and educational.

It's likely that you have a large pet-supply store or a privately owned pet shop close to your home. You can browse a range of food, supplies, and specialty items at these stores and find someone on staff to give you guidance about the different products.

Find out if there's an AKC all-breed dog show in your area. Not only are dog shows great places to meet other Chihuahua people but the big shows usually have a variety of trade stands or booths that cater to every need of the modern Chihuahua and every whim of his doting owners.

Collar and Leash

Purchase a soft buckle collar and a lightweight leash (6 feet long and a ½-inch thick) with a small but sturdy clasp. Many trainers prefer harnesses when working with Toy breeds to protect the dogs' delicate chest and torso. If you opt for

Think Like a Chihuahua

The best way to puppy-proof your home is to think like a Chihuahua, and get down on all fours to see the world from your puppy's perspective. Your Chihuahua may be able to see things that you never realized he could, such as stray rubber bands, a half-eaten candy bar under the couch, or a frayed wire laying across the carpet. It's up to you to predict what trouble your Chihuahua will be tempted to get into, so that you can prevent it before it happens.

How Many Shots Before Getting Social?

Often breeders and veterinarians advise new puppy owners to keep puppies at home until their vaccination schedule is complete. Puppies can be as old as four months by the time their vaccination course is complete, which is very late to start socializing a puppy with the outside world. Instead, an owner should be cautious about which dogs the puppy meets. Always restrict your Chihuahua's access to unknown dogs so that you're certain he only meets dogs that have been fully vaccinated. While it's important to keep the puppy away from strange, possibly unvaccinated dogs before he is fully vaccinated, you also don't want to compromise his socialization.

a collar, make sure it's comfortable on the dog and neither too tight nor too loose. Because the Chihuahua's neck is often wider than his head, it's possible that a regular buckle collar will easily slip over the dog's head. A safer option for training purposes is a martingale collar, which is a double-looped collar with the dog's head in one loop and the leash attached to the second loop. The first loop tightens as the leash pulls on the second loop. Never leave a martingale collar on the dog when you're not training with him, as it can easily get caught on objects and choke the dog.

Food Bowls

Stainless steel bowls are the most sensible feeding dishes to purchase, and you'll need to buy the smallest ones available. It's wise to purchase at least four bowls for your dog, so that you can keep one set outdoors and one indoors. Stainless steel is dishwasher safe, which is the best way to sanitize your dog's bowls. Of course, pet-supply stores have many kinds of dog bowls for sale, many of which are very attractive and fun. If you purchase plastic or ceramic bowls, make sure you clean them thoroughly as they can harbor harmful bacteria, and discard them when they wear out or begin to chip.

Grooming Supplies

Even though the Chihuahua is not much of a grooming challenge—compared to an Afghan Hound or a Cocker Spaniel, for example—you still need to purchase quality grooming equipment. You'll want to buy a gentle brush and a small rubber curry comb for your Chihuahua puppy. Once the puppy's adult coat comes in, you'll need to purchase a couple of extra tools, such as a medium-toothed comb to help remove mats and tangles from long coats and a chamois grooming glove to keep smooth coats shiny; but at this early stage, a basic brush and curry comb are all you'll need. You will also need canine nail clippers, along with some common household items such as cotton balls and extra towels. Round up your grooming supplies along with some dog shampoo and dental-care items—a dog toothbrush and dog toothpaste.

Toys

Don't forget to purchase some safe chew toys for your puppy. As teething can last for months, it will seem at first that your puppy's only train of thought is his mouth. Select a few different small toys to offer your Chihuahua. A squeaky toy made of hard rubber, a cuddly stuffed toy, and a hard nylon bone or teething ring will provide enough options in the beginning. Also, purchase something the puppy can chase and fetch, like a small ball or flying disk. Keep safety foremost in your mind when selecting toys and always supervise the puppy when playing with new toys. Avoid toys with removable parts and toys that are too large, as well as tug toys, which may loosen the Chi's little teeth.

Bedding

There are two options for sleeping accommodations, and you will likely want to take advantage of both. A dog bed, which can be as simple as a pillow or as elaborate as a canopy dollhouse bed, is essential for daytime naps. While the puppy is still house-training, you're wiser to go with something simple (and machine-washable!) so he doesn't soil his fancy bedding. Once he's older, you can purchase something prettier and more fancy. The second option, a crate, will serve as your puppy's "den" and is undoubtedly the most reliable house-training tool. Instinctually, dogs do not like to soil where they sleep, so once the puppy is accustomed to sleeping overnight in the crate, he will accept the den as his bed

Though your Chihuahua is the smallest dog around, he still needs all the essential supplies: dog bowls, leashes, a collar, grooming supplies, bedding, and toys. Don't skimp on quality—get the best products you can afford for your Chihuahua and they will last a long time.

and will not soil it. Purchase the smallest crate possible for the Chihuahua, which will suffice for the dog as a puppy and as an adult. Buy a durable crate that can be easily washed or wiped down. Both the fiberglass airline style and the traditional wire crate can be lined with comfortable soft bedding that can be washed frequently. Be sure to keep your dog's bedding clean and dry. When the puppy has an accident in the crate—it's going to happen—be prepared to disinfect it with a dog-safe cleaner.

CHI-PROOFING

Don't let the Chihuahua's tiny size fool you: he's capable of super-sized mischief! To puppy-proof your house, think like a toddler and crawl around your home. See the house and yard from a height of four inches, and consider which everyday household items aren't as harmless as they first appear. Waste baskets and kitchen garbage cans, houseplants, bathroom cabinets, low drawers, tablecloths, and dangling curtains are invitations to a Chihuahua with mischief on his mind. Even more dangerous to a curious, teething puppy are electrical cords, which should be hidden and protected from his searching teeth and paws. A Chihuahua's tiny teeth can easily bite into an electrical cable, causing a possibly fatal accident. Many cleaning agents, gardening aids, and other household chemicals contain substances that are poisonous, so don't store them in low cabinets or on the floor. Antifreeze, for example, is especially dangerous; just a few sweet-tasting drops can kill a small dog.

Keeping your Chihuahua safe can be a full-time occupation if you don't take precautions ahead of time. Because this puppy is tiny, fast, and too clever for his

Your Chihuahua will quickly get bored and destructive if left alone for too long. Provide your Chi with a variety of toys to keep him occupied and away from off-limit items.

Carrying Your Chi

Learn how to properly and safely carry your Chihuahua around. Hold him close against you, and never let him dangle without support. Center the Chihuahua's chest in one hand, with your middle fingers underneath him and your thumb and pinkie on either side of his body, and hold him close against your side. Do not squeeze the dog's front legs together or stick your fingers between his body and elbows, as this can harm his delicate frame.

own good, you have to make sure that he can't squeeze through tiny crevices in your walls, behind appliances, or inside furniture, such as recliners, box springs, or sofas. Puppy-proofing is never finished; it's an ongoing chore.

Look into purchasing puppy gates, playpens, and/or exercise pens to confine your roaming Chihuahua to safe, puppy-proofed areas. Manufacturers sell these products with close spokes to prevent small dogs from slipping through them. Some puppy gates are expandable and fit into the framework of a door and others are self-standing. Choose the best style and design for your home.

INTRODUCTIONS AT HOME

As tempted as you may be to tuck your new Chihuahua puppy in the crook of your arm and start introducing him to your neighbors, family, and coworkers, the "Look, I got a new puppy" tour is not on the first day's agenda. In fact, you should wait a few days for your puppy to settle into his new surroundings and get to know you and your family first. The Chihuahua's first few days are best spent quietly at home with as little commotion as possible. If you selected the most outgoing puppy in the litter, it's possible that when he first arrives in the unfamiliar surroundings of your home, he will lack a bit of the confidence that impressed you at the breeder's.

Keep Toys New

Here's a quick toy tip: only offer your Chihuahua two or three toys to play with. If you overwhelm your Chi with lots of toys all at once, he'll quickly get bored with all of them. Rotate the two or three toys every few days (or each week), and your Chihuahua will be excited to play with something new!

With no familiar sights, sounds, or smells, he's suddenly dealing with a world that is completely new to him. Be affectionate and gently encouraging to build up his confidence. In a few days, he'll start to relax into his usual outgoing personality.

Make a point to expose your puppy to the various noises that he will encounter around your house. Your goal isn't to upset or scare the puppy by suddenly blaring a radio, but instead to allow him near running appliances so he becomes accustomed and familiar with the many common noises around the house. While the pup is chewing on a toy in the kitchen, turn on the microwave, the dishwasher, or the blender. Ignore the puppy and go about your chores. In the bathroom, let him hear the toilet flush, the shower run, the fan buzz, and the hair dryer blowing away. Let the puppy hear the washer and dryer, the television, the doorbell, and your computer warming up. Your pup will soon become used to all of the noises we are surrounded with and not even bat an eyelash.

You'll know your puppy is comfortable in your home when he starts bossing you, your children, and even the family cat around. Once that day arrives, and he's feeling typically full of himself, you can introduce him to neighbors and friends. If you do have children or a cat, here's a word of caution. Always carefully supervise any introductions of your puppy with kids or other pets. Youngsters, even well-behaved ones, can all too easily hurt a puppy as tiny as the Chihuahua. A pup this petite, possibly weighing less than a pound, is especially fragile.

Regarding other family pets, be careful and watchful of all interactions with the puppy, as most cats and other dogs will undoubtedly be many times the size of a Chihuahua. When properly introduced, most Chihuahuas get along well with other animals, but close supervision is required to ensure that your puppy is safe and doesn't have a bad experience. Your Chihuahua puppy can very easily be injured by other pets, so watch your pup like a mama hawk.

THE SOCIAL CHIHUAHUA

Once his confidence in his surroundings is secure, your Chihuahua will be ready to spread his wings and mix and mingle like a social butterfly. Canine behaviorists contend that the most critical imprinting period in a dog's life are the first twelve weeks. Because many Chihuahua puppies will be arriving at their new homes between ten and twelve weeks of age, a good breeder will have given the puppy lots of human interaction and stimulation. It's even more important that you continue that socialization as soon as you bring your puppy home.

New owners should place socialization on the top of their "to-do" lists. Take your Chihuahua out and about to dog-friendly places, not just to the dog park, the pet store, and local yappy hours, but also to people places, too. With a pup as small as this, it's easy to carry him to the salon, the coffee shop, the mall, food stores, and home-improvement centers. Of course, depending on the management, you may have to hang out in the parking lot, but remember, when it comes to toting your tot into stores and restaurants, it's always easier to ask for forgiveness than permission. And who can resist that adorable Chihuahua face!

Consider the Microchip

In addition to a dog collar and ID tag, think about having your veterinarian insert a microchip in your dog to help find him if he ever gets lost. When scanned, the microchip will show your dog's unique microchip number so that your Chihuahua can be returned to you as soon as possible. Go to www.akccar.org to learn more about the nonprofit American Kennel Club Companion Animal Recovery (AKC CAR) pet recovery system.

Since 1995, the AKC CAR recovery service has been selected by millions of dog owners who are grateful for the peace of mind and service that AKC CAR offers.

Introduce your new Chihuahua to other pets slowly, and watch their interactions carefully. Keep all meetings calm and conflict-free so that your Chihuahua's first experiences with other pets are positive.

For the first three weeks, set a goal of three new places a week. Take your Chihuahua with you for a few hours while running errands on the weekend. Don't overdo it, though, because the puppy still needs his rest and you don't want to deprive him of his necessary siestas. Meeting lots of new people—as individuals, in couples, or in small groups—makes for a well-socialized dog.

Always supervise interactions between your puppy and new people. Some people don't know how to approach a dog, so be proactive in advising them. Ask people to squat down low and not to lean over the dog. Getting close to the dog's level makes the dog more confident and less fearful of being squashed by the giant hovering over him. Have people offer the back of their hand for the pup to sniff. Once the puppy has thoroughly tested their scents, then they can give your Chi a rub under his chin or on his chest. Discourage people from patting the dog's head because dogs don't like to be touched where they can't see, and the Chihuahua's head is extremely fragile (especially if the molera, or soft spot, is present).

Make socializing fun for your puppy. Give each new visitor a treat to share with the puppy after he or she has said hello. Be wary of well-meaning kids! Children get very excited when meeting Chihuahuas because they're so tiny and cute. Always be in control. Nicely but firmly tell children to go easy, use a quiet voice, and only approach the puppy one at a time. Never let a crowd of children surround your Chihuahua at once, as this can be very overwhelming for the puppy. Meeting one or two people at a time is fun—a crowd is never fun, especially of boisterous little people, no matter how many treats are offered.

Getting social with your Chihuahua is not simple recreation, but rather a vital and necessary part of growing up. Puppies that are not socialized at a young age can develop behavior problems as they mature, including shyness, separation anxiety, fear biting, and aggression. Socialization means the difference between a skittish, unapproachable, yappy lapdog and a polite, biddable, fun-to-be-around companion dog. For an owner, a happy, well-adjusted dog is a source of pride and pleasure, far better than an insurance risk on a leash that lunges at passing Poodles and strolling babies.

Socialization should not stop with puppyhood. Continue to introduce your Chihuahua to new people and places throughout his life to keep him confident and friendly.

At a Glance ...

Don't be overwhelmed by the amount of dog products at your local pet store. Concentrate on the essentials: food bowls, a collar, a leash, a crate, a bed, and a few chew toys. You can slowly add to your Chihuahua's possessions as he grows.

· ·

The world looks very different from four inches off the ground! Get down on your hands and knees to see the world from your Chihuahua's perspective. Puppy-proof everything in reach, including electrical wires, dangling curtains, and low drawers and cupboards.

· ·

Socialization is a must for every dog. Once you introduce your Chihuahua to your home, begin to slowly introduce him to the world by running errands with him and introducing him to new people and experiences.

CHAPTER FIVE

Chihuahua Education

It's never too early to start your puppy's education. From the day he comes into your home, you can begin teaching him right from wrong. That is, what humans think is right and wrong, which is not necessarily what canines think. Our rules don't make a lot of sense to dogs, but it's our job as teachers to instill in them a sense of what is expected.

A puppy's attention span passes in a blink, so keep your pup's first lessons short and fun. The first lessons, in fact, should be games. For

Busting Boredom

A dull daily existence can keep a good Chihuahua down. Enhance your Chi's life by providing stimulation in the form of interactive toys. The most popular are rubber toys with holes to fill with treats or soft toys dabbed in peanut butter, but you can also entertain your Chi with a remote-controlled toy he can chase and attack. You may even want to experiment with some cat toys that are appropriately sized for the Chihuahua. On weeknights, you should consider making your Chi's mealtime fun by having him find his kibble around the kitchen floor or having him extract it from a new rubber toy. These puzzle toys are great mental and physical stimulation for your Chi, welcome for growing puppies and slowing seniors.

canines, "play" is more than fun and games—it's a way of learning. Your puppy played with his mother and littermates, and through those games he learned some life lessons, such as when his bite was too hard, why it's easier to follow, and what a growl or snarl means.

MAKE LEARNING FUN

Puppies naturally need a leader, which some trainers attribute to canine pack instinct. While your pup was reared by his dam, she was his leader: the big, strong one who provided food, warmth, and direction. Mom had all the answers. Now that your Chihuahua is in your care, you must become his pack leader, the provider of all his needs. A simple game of "follow the leader" can reinforce this basic lesson with the puppy. Grab a tasty treat and walk from room to room, calling your puppy's name. As he follows you from one room to the next, give him a treat and say "good boy" or "good girl." This game also helps teach the puppy his name.

Another fun game for your puppy is "come to me." Wait until your puppy is sitting on one side of the room or in the next room. Enter the room, clap your hands, and happily say, "Sammy, come to me!" When he comes barreling toward you, give him a treat and lots of crazy, silly praise. The puppy is learning to recognize his name and you're teaching him that coming to you leads to good things

Did You Know?

The modern Chihuahua is much smaller than its Mexican ancestor, the Techichi. It is believed that the Chinese Crested, brought from Asia to Alaska across the Bering Strait, is responsible for the Chihuahua's petite size and shorter hair.

Many common dog toys will be too large for your Chihuahua. Purchase toys made for small dogs or even cat toys. These will be easier for your petite Chi to handle.

Make Your Puppy a S.T.A.R.

The American Kennel Club has a great program for new puppy owners called the S.T.A.R. Puppy® Program, which is dedicated to rewarding puppies that get off to a good start by completing a basic training class. S.T.A.R. stands for: Socialization, Training, Activity, and Responsibility.

You must enroll in a six-week puppy-training course with an AKC-approved evaluator. When the class is finished, the evaluator will test your puppy on all the training taught during the course, such as being free of aggression toward people and other puppies in the class, tolerating a collar or body harness, allowing his owner to take away a treat or toy, and sitting and coming on command.

If your puppy passes the test, he will receive a certificate and a medal. You and your puppy will also be listed in the AKC S.T.A.R. Puppy records. To learn more about the AKC S.T.A.R. Puppy Program or to find an approved evaluator near you, check out www.akc.org/starpuppy.

(such as food treats and petting). Never call your puppy to you to correct him. He needs to associate coming when called with praise, not punishment.

Here's the "let's get dressed" game. Begin simply by placing a small buckle collar around your pup's neck, not too tightly, but not so loosely that he can squirm out of it or get it caught on things. Just put it on for a few minutes and let him walk around the house or yard. The next day, leave the collar on for bit longer until your puppy feels comfortable in his first item of "clothing." When he's older, he can wear a sweater or even booties to keep him warm in the winter!

Now, how about a fun game of "chase the leash"? Take a small lightweight leash and walk in front of him dragging it on the floor. Let him sniff and chase, but don't let him chew it. Once he's not afraid of the leash, attach it to his collar. Be sure that the leash has a secure catch, yet is simple to attach and release as necessary. Let the puppy walk around the yard or the house dragging the leash around with you following him. The dog is getting used to the feel of a collar and leash with no pressure or tugging from you.

The next game—or lesson, if you must—is an extension of the above. Place the collar and leash on the puppy, and after letting him wander around the yard or house for a while, pick up the leash and let him lead you around. For the first few lessons, take it easy, be in no hurry, and just enjoy the puppy's company.

KEEP IT POSITIVE

The key to effective puppy training is positive reinforcement. Positive reinforcement takes into account your puppy's favorite things: treats and praise. When your puppy does something good, reward him with a treat and lots of hugs,

kisses, and belly rubs. Your Chihuahua will naturally want to repeat the behavior because he wants to receive more treats and praise.

This same type of training can be applied to bad behavior. When your puppy does something negative, such as digging through the trash or barking, remind yourself that he does these things because they make him feel good, not because he is purposely doing something bad to spite you. Dogs don't have ulterior motives. Take your puppy's wrongdoings simply for what they are—fun explorations of the world around him. Do not yell or overreact. Ignore the dog's bad behavior—the worst punishment for the attention-seeking Chi—and vow to be more vigilant in catching your puppy in the act so you can teach him what is and is not acceptable behavior around the house.

PUPPY KINDERGARTEN

The first training class that you can enroll your puppy in is a puppy socialization class, often called "puppy kindergarten." Puppy kindergarten is a great way to get your puppy into the real world for some much-needed socialization. Your puppy will have the chance to learn how to interact with other dogs and people. He'll also be introduced to walking on a leash and some of the basic training cues such as *sit* and *heel*. A course instructor will evaluate all of the puppies in the class and look for any shy or aggressive tendencies in your pup. Puppy kindergarten is a great opportunity to ask the instructor lots of questions about training and puppy care. Your questions will be rewarded with the advice of a trained professional—there's no better way to get your Chihuahua started on the right foot!

To find a puppy kindergarten class near you, ask your veterinarian, breeder, local breed club, or local pet-supply store for recommendations. Visit a class or two before signing up to find the best fit for you and your Chihuahua puppy.

CRATE THINGS HAPPEN!

Introducing your puppy to his crate should be an easy, gradual process. Begin by placing the crate in an area of the house where the puppy spends much of his time. Place a nice, plush towel in the bottom of the crate and leave the door open. At first, you can let the pup explore the crate as he wishes. If he carries a toy into the crate or takes a mini siesta there, you're making great progress. If he completely ignores the crate, sit between him and the crate, take a little piece of cheese or a treat and use it to get his attention. Let him nibble it and then toss it into the crate. Once he's in the crate, toss him a second treat. Try introducing him to a new squeaky toy while he's inside. He'll soon think that great stuff happens when he's in there!

An animal training method that is popular among dog trainers is clicker training. First used by dolphin trainers, clicker training uses a small handheld device that emits a short clicking sound when pressed. Trainers will "mark" a good behavior by clicking the device whenever the animal performs the desired behavior. The "mark" is reinforced with a treat immediately following the clicking sound. Dogs quickly learn that good behavior prompts the clicking sound, and they recognize that a treat is soon to follow. Clicker training helps dogs pinpoint the exact behavior that will earn them a reward, and it encourages them to repeat the behavior again and again.

What's in a Name?

You may have had your Chihuahua's name picked out from day one or you may want to get to know your puppy for a few days or weeks before deciding on the perfect name for him. When choosing a name for your pup, the best advice is to keep it simple. A one- or two-syllable name is much easier for your dog to learn and remember than a long, tongue-twisting mouthful. It's also helpful to avoid names that sound like common training cues such as *sit*, *stay*, or *come*. Names such as Mitt, Faye, or Plum will only confuse your Chi when it comes time for more advanced training.

Within a couple of days, close the door of the crate while he's chewing on a toy or snoozing. Read or play a few rounds of Angry Birds while remaining within your puppy's eyeshot. Gradually lengthen the amount of time that he's in the crate with the door closed. Once he gets used to being in a closed crate, you can leave the room and go about doing your everyday chores. Chihuahuas generally like to burrow in a towel or blanket in their crates, especially for their mid-morning, mid-afternoon, and mid-evening cat naps.

ONE BRICK AT A TIME

Mexico City wasn't built in a day! Be patient, stay positive, and take basic training one step at a time. Each training lesson—game, behavior, or cue—is another brick in the wall, and trust is the cement. The more you bond with your Chihuahua, gaining his complete trust and loyalty, the better behaved your dog will be. Don't attempt to rush your Chihuahua puppy's training: it's one step, one brick, and one lesson at a time.

At a Glance ...

Don't try to teach your Chihuahua formal obedience training right away. Start out with simple lessons in the form of games, such as teaching your Chihuahua his name, to come when called, and to get used to wearing a collar and leash.

The most effective form of dog training is through positive reinforcement. When your puppy does something good, praise him by clapping your hands, tossing him a treat, and giving him lots of rubs and pets. He'll naturally repeat the good behavior because he wants the reward!

Once your puppy has received all his vaccinations, sign up for a puppy kindergarten class. Puppy kindergarten is a great way to socialize your pup and have him interact with other puppies and a variety of new people.

CHAPTER SIX

House-Training Your Chi

One of the most prevalent misconceptions about Chihuahuas, and Toy dogs in general, is that they are difficult to house-train. Toy dogs are no easier or more difficult to teach than larger dogs; in fact, Toy dogs are not the stubborn ones, but rather, it's the Toy-dog owners! That's not to say that Chihuahua owners aren't fully committed to their dogs; clearly they're completely devoted to their tiny charges. However, babying the Chihuahua often

leads to a poorly behaved, untrained companion. A spoiled Toy dog—imagine that! Owners typically make excuses for their babies' temperamental behavior or little accidents. Toy-dog owners must treat their canines as if they were normal-sized dogs, not precious ornaments or fragile accessories. A Chihuahua thinks and acts like a dog, because he is one. Dogs expect leadership and structure in their lives, and their owners must provide it.

HOUSE RULES

When it comes to house-training, Chihuahua owners rarely think it's a big deal. That may be simply because a four-month-old Chihuahua's little accident is just that, little—nothing a tissue or paper towel can't clean up in a few seconds. Owners of Labradors or Boxers, for example, take house-training much more seriously because the mess is considerably worse! Begin your house-training routine with conviction: an accident is an accident, regardless of the size of your dog.

If you're lucky enough to have acquired a Chihuahua from a breeder who began house-training for you, then you should continue using the same training method as the breeder. Most breeders use crate-training, which is the preferred

A PIECE OF HISTORY

The Chihuahua is descended from an ancient Mesoamerican breed of dog called the Techichi, raised originally by the Toltec civilization in what is now modern-day Mexico. The Techichi existed within the Toltec culture as early as the 9th century AD.

On the Spot!

Many trainers believe that introducing a simple command can be helpful for house-training. "Business," "potty," or "hurry up" may work for your Chihuahua, or choose one of your own. Always praise the pup when he goes in the desired place. However, if you catch your pup going in the wrong spot, make a loud noise to startle him, pick him up, and quickly bring him to his place (newspaper, litter box, or outside), and then say "Good dog." Never reprimand a puppy for the mess you just found on the floor. He will not connect your unhappiness and the correction with anything that he did; corrections after the fact only serve to confuse the puppy and weaken his trust in his favorite person.

method for most dogs and their owners. Remember that house-training is about the house first, and your house is completely different from the breeder's. The place smells completely different. Doors aren't in the same places, the hallways and floors are unfamiliar, and your family may go to bed and rise at different times. It will undoubtedly take a little time for the semi-housebroken Chi to learn the rules of the house and adapt to his new home.

THE BEST METHOD?

With a dog as small as the Chihuahua, owners have a few house-training methods to choose from. You must consider your living space, your house-training expectations, and your Chihuahua's house-training history before selecting one method over another. No method is better than another—the keys to successful house-training are patience, consistency, and vigilance.

Keep It Clean

Your role as a Chihuahua owner is not only as leader and teacher, but also chief housekeeper. Accidents will happen when house-training your puppy. Don't underestimate the power of that little nose. If a dog relieves himself in the wrong place, you must use a safe cleaner to neutralize the odor. If your Chi can smell his urine, he will want to use that particular place again. Stock up on odor-neutralizing cleansers and absorbent paper towels. When your puppy is old enough to be exercised in public places, always carry a small plastic bag so that any droppings can be removed and thrown away in the nearest trash can. It's the considerate thing to do; and in many places, it's the law.

PAPER TRAINING

Paper training may be the best option for city dwellers whose dogs don't have quick access to an outside area. A puppy in "gotta-go" mode cannot hold it while the elevator descends twenty floors or while you sprint down your six-floor walk-up.

Set up a series of baby gates or exercise pens to contain your puppy to a small area. Choose a place that is in a high-traffic area such as the kitchen (which is ideal because kitchens usually do not have carpet) so that he doesn't feel lonely or ostracized. Place his crate and food bowls in one corner of the area, and line the rest of the space with newspaper. After a day or so, you should notice that your puppy prefers to go to the bathroom in one general area of the space. Piece by piece, over a few days, slowly remove the surrounding pieces of paper until your Chihuahua is consistently relieving himself on one piece of paper. If he has an accident off the paper—no problem! Just add a piece of paper back to the area until he starts using one small area again.

Once he understands that the paper is the place for him to go, you can take down the exercise pens and slowly move the paper to the spot in the house where you want him to go on a regular basis. Don't move the paper too fast! An inch or two a day is plenty. Soon, your Chihuahua will be fully paper trained!

Paper training is also a useful option in the very early stages of house-training, even if it's not your first and last choice. Newspapers—three or four sheets thick—or puppy pee-pads should be placed by the door you normally use to go outside so that the dog learns to associate the paper with the exit to the out-doors. When he uses the paper, he should be praised. If you see your puppy doing his wee-wee dance by the door, whisk him up and take him outside. However, if possible, don't confuse your puppy with too many house-training methods at once. If you plan on house-training your Chihuahua to go to the bathroom outside, it is best not to paper-train him first. This will only confuse your Chihuahua as to where he should relieve himself. Remember, consistency is key, and a consistent, repetitive approach to house-training will be the most successful.

LITTER-BOX TRAINING

Litter-box training is very similar to paper training. While litter-box habits are not instinctual to a dog as they are to a cat, Toy dogs can very easily get used to the idea of using a litter box. Line the box with sheets of newspaper or litter and place the box by the door you normally use to go outside. Place the pup in the box whenever he shows signs of having to relieve himself. Apartment dwellers often opt for litter boxes, as do owners who have to leave their dogs at home for long periods of time. It's a convenience for the owner, giving him or her peace of mind knowing that the dog is not at home "holding it" for eight hours.

CRATE-TRAINING

If you want your Chihuahua to relieve himself outside, select the spot and regularly take your puppy to the same spot for every potty break. In fact, you should have taken your puppy to his potty spot the moment you first brought him home from the breeder.

Crate-training is the gateway to outdoor training. Pet-supply stores offer a variety of styles and sizes of crates. The two most common types are airline crates, constructed of fiberglass with a plastic or metal door, and wire crates, which are more open, affording better ventilation and visibility. The crate should be small, only large enough for your Chihuahua to stand and turn around inside it. You don't want your Chihuahua to be able to go to the bathroom on one end of the crate and sleep on the other. A dog's natural instinct is not to soil the place where he sleeps, which is the foundation of the crate-training method.

Place the crate in the Chihuahua's favorite room, where he spends the most time, such as the kitchen or family room. Place a towel in the crate so that your pup is comfortable when he's napping. Eventually, you'll be able to place nicer,

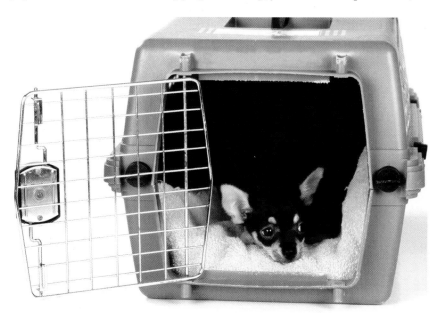

Your Chi's crate will become much more than a house-training tool. The crate will become your puppy's safe haven and relaxation place where he can go to be alone and feel protected when you're not around.

more comfortable bedding inside the crate, but until your Chihuahua is fully house-trained, stick with an easy-to-wash towel.

Put your puppy in his crate at night, during nap time, or whenever you can't keep a close watch on him, such as when you need to take a shower or run a few quick errands. Also, try feeding him a few meals inside the crate so that he associates it with good things. Never put your Chihuahua in his crate as a punishment. You want him to see his crate as a comfortable, relaxing, positive place. It should be his refuge, not a place of punishment.

Your Chihuahua will begin to view his crate as his den and he will understand that it's his sacred place for sleeping. Whenever you release your puppy from his crate, immediately take him outside to relieve himself. Puppies need to relieve themselves more frequently than adults. Hourly is the rule, so take your puppy and place him on the grass once an hour (unless he's sleeping). Bring him outside whenever you release him from his crate, especially after all meals and naps. Always keep both eyes and ears open because a youngster will not be able to wait those extra two or three minutes until it is convenient for you to let him out. If you delay, accidents will certainly happen, so be ready.

Whenever you take your puppy outside to relieve himself, always use the same door so as not to confuse your pup. Your home seems massive and confusing to the tiny Chihuahua puppy. He won't remember how to get outside if you constantly use alternative routes to get him there. Use the same door to the outside every time, and try to use the same pathway through the house to get there.

Take your Chihuahua to the same potty spot each time you go outside, and use the same cue phrase repeatedly. Some popular choices include, "Go potty" or "Do your business." These habitual practices will help your puppy remember why he is outside in the first place. Be sure that your Chihuahua does his business before he gets distracted; once he relieves himself, then you can reward him with a free frolic around the backyard.

Gradually increase the amount of time your puppy spends in his crate. This will train him to "hold it" for longer periods of time. By four months old, your puppy should be able to spend three to four hours inside his crate; by five months, four or five hours, and by six months, six hours. Never keep your dog confined to his crate for longer than six hours unless it is at night when he is sleeping. If you can't be home to take your dog out for a quick walk and a potty break, enlist the help of a neighbor or dogsitter.

In time your puppy will learn that outside is the place to go to relieve himself. With consistency and vigilance, your clever Chihuahua will be house-trained in no time.

A Chihuahua's small size lends itself well to paper, litter-box, or backyard house-training. No matter which method you choose, stay consistent and your Chi will be house-trained in a matter of weeks.

THE HUMAN TOUCH

Spend quality time with your Chihuahua outside of house-training, petting him and talking to him. Chihuahuas need to feel connected with their humans. If the only time you pick up your Chihuahua is to move him from his mess to his crate or to extract him from danger or mischief, then you're not investing quality time with your puppy. Bonding with your Chihuahua reinforces the dog's trust in you and improves training and socialization. Make house-training, and all the time in between, fun and exciting for your puppy. This time in your puppy's life is one of discovery and learning that you should cherish and enjoy. When the right amount of time and effort is put into the method, house-training can be a simple lesson that your Chihuahua puppy will learn in a matter of weeks. Be patient and consistent, and your hard work and dedication will be rewarded with a well-behaved, house-trained pup!

Don't let your puppy get distracted until he goes to the bathroom in his designated potty spot. Once your puppy relieves himself, you can celebrate with some outside play and exploration.

At a Glance ...

The keys to successful house-training are patience, consistency, and vigilance. Remember that house-training is not a natural behavior for your puppy. You must take the time to teach your puppy what is expected of him and be consistent in your training methods.

Before deciding on a house-training method, consider your lifestyle and your home environment. Whichever method you choose, be consistent as not to confuse your Chihuahua.

The crate should be your puppy's personal den and sanctuary. Do not put your puppy in his crate as a punishment, but rather, use the crate as a tool to train your puppy to hold it until he has a chance to relieve himself outside.

CHAPTER SEVEN

Building Your Chihuahua's Skills

The hurdle that many Chihuahua owners face is a simple one: convincing the Chihuahua that obedience and good manners are his idea. No one would deny that the Chihuahua is one very bright little dog, but unlike a Golden Retriever or a Collie, the Chihuahua doesn't live to please his owner; rather, his curiosity and daring often get the better of him. He is an easily distracted, resourceful little dog that has Great Dane-sized ideas. Think big and train big!

Though Chihuahuas are easily totable, it's important that your Chi learn to walk politely on a leash and behave mannerly in public.

Approach the training of your Chihuahua as if you are training a normal-sized dog. As we've said, many loving Chihuahuans are guilty of letting their dogs go completely untrained, letting their tots run the house and ignore cues and rules. These folk believe that once the Chihuahua is house-trained, their job as an educator is done. Untrained Chihuahuas can be yippy, nippy nightmares in public, which obviously damages the breed's reputation. If you're a person who truly loves Chihuahuas, then be serious about your dog's training.

Training a free-thinking dog like the Chihuahua can be tricky. Given their independent nature, Chis don't actually believe they need their owners to solve problems. Owners therefore must approach training with authority and conviction, before the Chi decides to walk all over his noncommittal commander.

PERSONAL TRAINING PLAN

You should have a training plan from day one. Here are eight principles of Chihuahua training on which to base your own plan:

1. Brainwash the Chihuahua with praise! Use tasty, tiny treats to reward the dog whenever he obeys a cue or behaves appropriately. The fastest way to a Chihuahua's brain is through his stomach!

2. Be consistent. House rules and cues have absolute meanings and don't change on weekends or after a long day at work.

3. Exercise your dog! Chihuahuas are high-energy dogs, so help expend all of that energy before you attempt to teach your dog any lesson.

4. Keep training sessions short. Limit each lesson to three to five minutes maximum.

5. Location! Location! Location! For your dog's first lessons, choose a part of your house that is quiet and distraction-free. As you progress, choose different locations that add variety and distractions in your lessons.

6. Use a firm, steady voice. Reserve your high-pitched, happy voice for rewarding and praising.

7. Get noticed. Be sure you have your dog's complete attention before beginning a lesson.

8. Always end on a high note. Complete lessons by reviewing a cue that the puppy knows, and then release him with an "OK" and engage in some play.

When training a dog, especially one that thinks he's superior, consistency and follow-through make all the difference. It's essential to get your dog's full attention, with the help of tasty treats and a confident approach. The following training method uses food treats, although in time, you can wean your dog off these training aids and base your training solely on praise.

SIT

Many owners begin training with the *sit* cue because it is easiest to master, but it is also the most useful skill your Chihuahua will learn. A Chihuahua that obeys this cue will sit politely when he meets a new person, won't attempt to jump up on visitors, and will pay closer attention when you are reinforcing other mannerly behaviors.

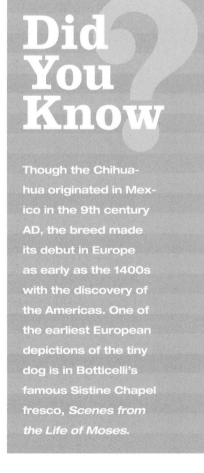

Did You Know?

Though the Chihuahua originated in Mexico in the 9th century AD, the breed made its debut in Europe as early as the 1400s with the discovery of the Americas. One of the earliest European depictions of the tiny dog is in Botticelli's famous Sistine Chapel fresco, *Scenes from the Life of Moses*.

Can Your Dog Pass the Canine Good Citizen® Test?

An AMERICAN KENNEL CLUB Program

Once your Chihuahua is ready for advanced training, you can start training him for the American Kennel Club Canine Good Citizen® Program. This program is for dogs that are trained to behave at home, out in the neighborhood, and in the city. It's easy and fun to do. Once your dog learns basic obedience and good canine manners, a CGC evaluator gives your dog ten basic tests. If he passes, he's awarded a Canine Good Citizen® certificate. Many trainers offer classes with the test as the final to graduate from the class. To find an evaluator in your area, go to www.akc.org/events/cgc/cgc_bystate.cfm.

Many therapy dogs and guide dogs are required to pass the Canine Good Citizen® test in order to help as working and service dogs in the community. There are ten specific skills that a dog must master in order to pass the Canine Good Citizen® test:

1. Let a friendly stranger approach and talk to his owner
2. Let a friendly stranger pet him
3. Be comfortable being groomed and examined by a friendly stranger
4. Walk on a leash and show that he is in control and not overly excited
5. Move through a crowd politely and confidently
6. Sit and stay on command
7. Come when called
8. Behave calmly around another dog
9. Not bark at or react to a surprise distraction
10. Show that he can be left with a trusted person away from his owner

In order to help your dog pass the AKC CGC test, first enroll him in basic training classes or a CGC training class. You can find classes and trainers near you by searching the AKC website. When you feel that your Chihuahua is ready to take the test, locate an AKC-approved CGC evaluator to set up a test date, or sign up for a test that is held at a local AKC dog show or training class. For more information about the AKC Canine Good Citizen® Program, visit www.akc.org/events.cgc.

Stand directly in front of your dog and lean over just enough to hold out a treat—do not kneel or sit down next to the dog. With the dog's leash in your left hand, raise the treat in your right hand and allow the dog to inspect it. Licking and sniffing are okay, but don't let him bite it or take it from your hand. You're simply building up his interest in the treat. Move the treat upward over the dog's head as you say "sit." Say it once with conviction so that the dog clearly recognizes the cue word. Limit your body language by keeping the leash as still as possible. Your Chihuahua should watch your hand as it rises over his head and look upward. As he continues to follow the treat over his head, he will automatically bend his knees and sit. When he sits, tell him "good boy," give him the treat, and lavish him with praise.

DOWN

Once your dog is proficient with the *sit* cue (and holding it for more than an instant), introduce the word "down." Understand that dogs consider the down position a submissive one, and small dogs don't like being any lower than they already are. Therefore, gentle training is important when teaching this cue.

With your Chihuahua by your left leg in the sit position, hold the leash in your left hand and a treat in your right. Reach down and place your left hand on top of the dog's shoulders (without pushing) and hold the treat under his nose, saying "down" in a quiet tone of voice. Slowly move the treat along the floor, in front of the dog and away from him, all the while talking gently. He will follow the treat, lowering himself down. When his elbows touch the floor, you can slowly release the treat and give soft praise. Too much praise can be misinterpreted as a release, and you want the dog to remain in the down position for a few seconds before getting up. Gradually, you can increase the time held in the down position.

Here's a quick tip about the down exercise: force and rough handling do not help teach a dog *down*. Small dogs are reluctant to assume this position, so forcing them by pushing on their shoulders or pulling their front feet out in front of them only makes matters worse. You can never force a dog to trust you!

STAY

Stay can be taught either in a sit or down position, whichever position is more comfortable for your dog. The difficulty of the *stay* cue is that you're not asking the dog to do anything: you're essentially asking him to wait for you to say "OK" and release him.

To begin, take the leash in your left hand and a treat in your right. Allow your Chi to lick the treat as you say "stay" while standing directly in front of the dog,

having moved from your position beside him. Silently count to five, then move back to your original position alongside him, allowing your dog to have the treat while giving him lavish praise.

Keep practicing the *stay* cue just as described for a few days, then gradually increase the distance between you and the dog, using your hand with the palm facing outward as an indication that he must stay. Soon you should be able to do this exercise without a leash, and your Chihuahua will begin to stay for longer periods of time. Always give lavish praise upon completion of the exercise for a job well done.

TAKE IT AND LEAVE IT

The *take it* and *leave it* cues come in handy when your curious pup picks up or gets into something he shouldn't, whether it's the kitchen trash, a poisonous plant, or a couch pillow. When you catch your Chihuahua red-handed, you want him to stop whatever he is doing immediately on your cue.

The first step is to teach your Chihuahua the *take it* cue. Take a treat in your right hand and have your puppy sit in front of you. Hold the treat in the palm of your hand and hold it in front of your dog's nose. When he tries to eat the treat, close your fingers around the treat so that he can't get it. Once your puppy calms himself, open your hand and let him take the treat as you say "take it." Keep repeating this exercise until your Chihuahua waits for you to say "take it" before he eats the treat.

Once your puppy has mastered *take it*, begin teaching *leave it*. Again, place a treat in the palm of your hand and hold it out to your dog. When he tries to take the treat, close your fingers around the treat and say "leave it." When he calms himself and waits, open your hand and say "take it," allowing him to take the treat. In time, your Chihuahua will begin to understand the meaning of "take it" and "leave it."

Once your Chihuahua starts to get the idea, try to use these cues in real-world situations, such as around the house or when you are on a walk. Place a treat or toy along your usual walking route. When you come across it, your puppy will most likely run over to investigate. When he does, say "leave it" and keep walking past the treat or toy. Be sure to give him a treat and lots of praise when he follows your cue. Don't forget to practice *take it* as well, letting him pick up and sniff new items, too—you don't want your puppy to feel like you are teasing him.

COME

Your Chihuahua must come when called—it could save his life. The idea is to cue him to return to you, always giving a treat and lots of praise when he does. Use the dog's name and the word "come" each time you give the cue. Choose a quiet,

A well-exercised Chihuahua makes a better student. You want him to be completely focused on you as you start your lesson.

distraction-free location to begin teaching the *come* cue. When you call the dog to "come," you have to ring it out like you're shouting "Bingo!" The word itself should make the dog giddy with anticipation for the promised reward.

Remember, don't ever call the dog to you for any reason other than to give him praise and a reward (or perhaps dinner!). Never call him to you to give him a correction; coming to you must always be a positive, happy experience. For instance, don't call the dog to you for his morning brushing or, even worse, nail clipping or bath. "Come" must be reserved for fun things!

Practice the *come* cue in the house and in the yard many times a day. Begin the lesson only a few feet away from the dog. Facing your dog, say, "Manny, come!" and give him a treat when he runs to you. Take a few more steps backward and repeat the exercise. Once he's reliably coming to you from just a few feet away, go farther and call him. If the dog is distracted by anything in his environment, stop the lesson. In the initial stages, avoid any situation in which the dog will not respond quickly and enthusiastically every time you call him.

Next, call him to you, and as soon as he reaches you, say "sit." When he does, give him a treat. Once you're sure that he is coming every time you call, begin practicing the exercise in different places, including places filled with distractions. Choose a moment when your Chihuahua is playing with a toy or investigating something interesting. Call him to you, and when he comes, shower him with praise and give him a special treat.

More important than any other lesson, the *come* cue can keep your Chihuahua out of danger. If the dog slips out of his collar or wiggles through a hole in

Reasons to Train Your Chihuahua

1. Working closely with your dog toward a common goal strengthens the bond between you and your Chihuahua.
2. Your dog will be safer and more receptive to your commands if he understands basic cues like *stay*, *come*, and *down*.
3. Other people will welcome your Chi's company if he's well behaved and under control, rather than snapping or growling at every new person or dog he meets.
4. Every dog, even a companion or lapdog, likes to feel that he has a purpose. Training will teach your Chihuahua to be more confident and personable.
5. Your Chihuahua learns that pleasing his favorite person only leads to positive things.
6. Basic obedience training reinforces your role as the leader of the household.
7. You and your dog can continue on to further pursuits, such as the Canine Good Citizen® Program, therapy work, and agility.
8. It's fun.

your fence, you want to be sure that the dog will come to you when called and not run out into traffic. Put as much effort into training your dog to *come* as you put into house-training.

HEEL

The word "heel" is the formal term for when a dog walks politely alongside his owner's heels. Precise heeling is an important part of obedience training, but it's not needed for everyday walking on a leash. All you need to achieve at this point in your puppy's life is a dog that will walk next to you without pulling. You don't want your dog choking himself, yanking against his collar, or possibly injuring his neck and throat. The Chihuahua is a very animated, busy little dog whose idea of a fun walk is likely running far ahead of his owner, swerving left and right, pulling, stopping, and weaving between his owner's legs until he trips. Let's convince the brainy Chihuahua that there's a better way.

Walking politely on leash requires that you control your dog and have a clear picture in your head of how you expect your dog to act. Before you teach this lesson, your dog should be comfortable with his leash and collar or harness. If your

No one likes to walk an out-of-control dog that wiggles and pulls on the leash like a fish on a line. Introduce your dog to a leash gradually and begin teaching the *heel* cue before taking your first walk.

Enrolling in a Group Class

Many Chi owners feel that homeschooling is the best option for their bright little charges. Even if you have an excellent dog-training school in your area, enrolling your young 2-pounder in a class with exuberant 60-pound Boxer or Golden Retriever adolescents can be anything but a positive educational experience for your petite pupil. Before enrolling in a class, visit the class without your dog in tow. Some schools have small-dog classes that are more appealing and safer for Chihuahuas. While observing the instructor, consider whether or not he or she is in control of the dogs and whether or not the safety of each dog is a primary concern. An unruly dog party is not what your Chihuahua needs.

Chihuahua gets overly excited whenever you reach for his leash, take a step back and work toward desensitizing the dog to his leash. Attach the leash to your dog and ignore him. No walk, no play, just attach the leash to the little man's collar and nothing more. The next day, attach the leash to his collar and hold it. Don't take a single step. Your goal is to have him stand next to you with a leash attached and remain calm, with his undivided attention on you, waiting for your next move. Practice the *sit* cue while he is on leash, but don't walk anywhere until he is routinely calm when you attach his leash.

Once he is calm and desensitized to the excitement of his leash, you are ready to begin walking. Attach the leash, stand quietly for a minute, and then say "sit." Grasp the leash in your left hand and tell the dog to sit next to your left leg. Hold the end of the leash in your right hand, and grasp the slack of the leash with your left. The dog should be waiting intently for your next move. Step forward with your right foot and say "let's go." To begin, just take three small steps, then cue him to sit again. Repeat this procedure until he carries out the task without pulling. Then, increase the number of steps to five, seven, and so on. Stop every few steps and say "sit." Keep praising your dog throughout the exercise, and at

the end of the training session let him enjoy himself with a free run and some playtime. After you've practiced this lesson for a few days, begin to go a bit farther and introduce turns, always keeping the speed moderate. Eventually you can vary the speed as well.

LIFE LESSONS

Basic obedience training is a must for every dog, no matter how big or small. Your tiny Chihuahua can become a big nuisance if he doesn't learn to abide by your rules and cues. Learning to *sit, stay,* and *come* on cue are the most important lessons that your dog will learn. These cues will keep your dog safe in dangerous situations, and you will feel all the more confident when taking your pup out into the world. A well-trained pup is a welcome pup!

Once you've mastered the basic cues, enroll your Chihuahua in a more advanced training course. There is always more to learn, and your Chi will welcome the extra time he gets to spend with you.

At a Glance ...

Your dog doesn't need advanced obedience training to be a well-behaved, mannerly dog. Practice the basic cues—*sit, stay, heel, take it* and *leave it,* and *come*—and you will have a reliable, friendly companion for a lifetime.

. . . .

Keep training fun. Your Chihuahua will respond more quickly and consistently to positive, reward-based training. Treats and praise are the fastest way to reach your Chi's mind and heart.

. . . .

Basic obedience training is about more than simply having a well-behaved dog—it can save your dog's life. Knowing that your dog will respond to your cues will not only keep your dog out of danger but it will also give you the confidence to introduce your dog to new people and places.

CHAPTER EIGHT

Chow for Your Chi

Eating is on most dogs' list of favorite things to do, and some Chihuahuas live for suppertime and all the other meals of the day. These "chowhounds" will be obvious to their owners: they will eat voraciously with no fuss, regardless of what's offered and when. It's easier if your Chihuahua is one of the more sensible, self-limiting eaters that will only eat as much as he needs at any given time. Owners with multiple Chihuahuas (or other dogs) will have to

There is a variety of treats available, so choose a healthy one made for small dogs. Human foods, such as plain popcorn, cheese, and pieces of hot dog, make great treats in a pinch, too.

be vigilant to make sure each little guy or gal is getting his or her portion.

Discuss your pup's nutritional needs with your veterinarian. Your doggy doctor is the most qualified person to determine the ideal diet for your Chi based on his or her observation and best judgment. No two Chihuahuas are the same, and some dogs will require more food than others to sustain themselves.

MEALTIME!

It's most appropriate to discuss diet and nutrition based on your Chihuahua's age. Puppies require more frequent meals than adults. Adults require a maintenance diet that is balanced and nutritious.

Once a puppy has been weaned, he should eat four or five times daily. All major dog-food manufacturers produce puppy food in both wet food (canned) and dry food (kibble). Most breeders recommend feeding the Chihuahua a combination of both. Add a little warm water to the dry puppy food when introducing it to the puppy. If the breeder warns you about hypoglycemia (low blood sugar) in your puppy, you will need to feed the puppy smaller portions at more frequent intervals.

At four to six months of age, a puppy should eat three times a day, more or less like people do. Once a puppy is eight months old, he is considered an adult and should be fed twice daily. Chihuahuas prefer structure, so if possible, feed your dog at the same time each day, usually in the morning and in the early evening.

A PIECE OF HISTORY

Before World War II, "dog food" was basically a combination of table scraps, leftover meats, and cheap ingredients such as cornmeal, grains, and cereal products. With the introduction of canned and dehydrated pet food in the 1940s, the commercial dog-food business began to gain popularity and variety. In the 1960s and 1970s, associations such as the National Research Council (NRC), the Animal Protection Institute (API), and the Association of American Feed Control Officials (AAFCO) began testing pet foods for "balance" and "completeness." By the 1980s, pet food became more as we recognize it today, introducing a variety of lifestage formulas, consistency types, and launching an industry that today earns over $20 billion a year.

By eight to ten years of age, depending on activity level, senior Chihuahuas require a change in diet. Portion the senior's food into three or four meals, not increasing his total amount per day. Seniors become less active as they age and additional calories are unwelcome. Senior foods usually include increased protein as well as antioxidants, such as vitamin E and beta carotene, recommended to boost immune-system function.

Most premium dog-food brands now help dog owners decide what's best for their dogs by formulating recipes for specific age groups and lifestyles. Puppies require a diet very different from that of adult and senior dogs. Due to their fast growth and physical development, puppies require a diet that includes more protein and fat, the key ingredients that support growth and high-energy lifestyles. Adults and seniors, on the other hand, have reached their mature size and body weight, and simply require a formula based on maintenance. These food formulas contain more nutrients and less calories, the perfect combination for your aging Chihuahua. These different lifestage formulas will help guide you to the right food choice for your Chihuahua.

FOOD CHOICE

There is an enormous range of dog foods available at pet stores and supply outlets. Not all foods are made equal, so put on your reading glasses and inspect the label. You want to see a high-quality protein as the first ingredient: chicken, beef, fish, or lamb, as opposed to a by-product or grain meal. Given the Chihuahua's small food intake, even the most expensive, organic, natural dog foods are considered affordable by most dog owners.

Major pet-food manufacturers in the United States boast scientifically formulated, complete and balanced foods. All store-bought dog foods in the country must first be tested by the Association of American Feed Control Officials

In multi-Chihuahua households, it's important to monitor mealtime to make sure each dog is eating his portion. Feed your dogs separately to be sure each Chi has enough uninterrupted time to eat.

Cooking for Your Chihuahua

One of the latest trends for dog owners is cooking for their dogs. If you're inclined to take on your dog's culinary duties, your Chi will love you for it! No matter how well processed and balanced commercial brands are, nothing compares to a fresh, home-cooked chicken, fish, or beef stew! Before you pursue this course, do your homework. Dogs need a properly balanced diet of protein, carbohydrates, vitamins, minerals, and fats. While canines are carnivores and their diet should include no less than 33 percent lean protein, they also require vegetables, fruits, and grains to have a balanced diet. Consult with your veterinarian or a veterinary nutritionist before donning your apron and firing up the stove.

(AAFCO). The AAFCO requires manufacturers to include a variety of ingredients in pet foods before they can claim themselves to be "complete and balanced." The nutrition and ingredient labels on dog-food packaging reveal the components of the food in descending order of weight or amount. Discuss with your veterinarian, breeder, or veterinary nutritionist what's best for your Chihuahua based on his age, weight, and lifestyle. Here are a few types of nutrients you will find on most dog-food labels:

• **Carbohydrates:** For active, youthful Chihuahuas, carbohydrates act as the primary energy source. They are broken down and converted into sugars in your dog's bloodstream.

• **Fats:** When carbohydrates aren't enough, fats are converted and broken down into secondary energy resources. Extra fats are stored in the body and help in the production of hormones and nervous-system function.

• **Proteins:** Extremely important for growing puppies, proteins help generate and repair muscle, bone, and other body tissues. They are also important in adult and senior diets to support immune-system function. Beware of too much protein, however, as it can cause skin irritations and/or kidney problems.

• **Vitamins:** Additional resources of nutrition, vitamins help stimulate growth, healing, and muscular- and nervous-system function in your Chihuahua.

• **Water:** Ample water is vital for all dogs and should be available at all times. Your Chihuahua's daily water intake keeps him hydrated and washes away excess waste in your dog's body. It also helps in the digestion and absorption of all food nutrients and ingredients.

If your Chihuahua is eating his food consistently, and he's looking healthy and remains energetic, there's no need to make adjustments to his diet. When changes are required, make them gradually and carefully. You may notice that your dog has become finicky with a certain food. Just as with people, dogs' palates can change over time, and a food that your Chi was eating with gusto at four months of age may be boring and unappealing a few months later. Likewise, if

your dog's coat is lacking sheen or body, or if your dog is acting sluggish, it's a good idea to try a different food. Never change suddenly from one food to another or your Chihuahua is likely to get an upset tummy. Introduce a new brand of food gradually over a few days until the old brand is phased out. There is usually no harm at all in changing the variety of the food while staying with the same brand. This can add some variety to the diet, or you might prefer to add a little flavored low-salt stock to tempt his taste buds.

There are several ways you can spice up your Chi's everyday kibble to make it more appetizing. Try adding a little chicken broth to soften the food or mix in a scoop of wet food. You can even add a few cooked veggies.

DRY, WET, SEMI-MOIST—OH, MY!

In addition to the different lifestage formulas currently available, most manufacturers offer dog food in several different types: dry, wet, and semi-moist. Again, depending on your dog's age, physical needs, and lifestyle, one type of food (or a combination of two) may be better for your Chihuahua than another. Seek the advice of your breeder or veterinarian to help you decide which is best for your energetic Chi.

Dry (Kibble): Recommended by most veterinarians, the rough consistency of dry food helps clean a dog's teeth of plaque and tartar. It is also the most economical choice of all the dog-food types. Should you decide to feed dry food, be sure to read the feeding instructions, though your Chi may eat less than the label recommends for small dogs. When selecting a dry food for your dog, keep in mind that you want a "small bite" or "small breed" variety because a Chihuahua cannot eat normal-sized pellets. Dry kibble needs to be moistened, especially for youngsters. Some Chis like their food moistened and some do not. Dry food

Go Natural!

Fresh dog foods can be found in the refrigerator section at pet-supply stores. These specialty "natural" foods feature high-quality protein sources, such as chicken, turkey, fish, and beef, prepared with minimal processing and no preservatives. Certain brands of natural foods have higher percentages of proteins and are free of grains, starches, and other fillers, boasting added antioxidants and Omega fatty acids. More easily digestible than other foods, fresh varieties are a godsend for picky eaters and dogs with allergies or special diets.

should also be stored carefully, bearing in mind that its vitamin value declines if not used fairly quickly, usually within about three months. Don't buy huge sacks unless you have a whole clan of Chihuahuas. It is essential that a plentiful supply of fresh water is available for your dog, especially when feeding dry foods.

Wet (Canned): Wet food, which comes prepackaged in cans, contains the choicest cuts of meats and vegetables doused in a hearty portion of tasty gravy. Ideal for picky eaters, canned food has a long shelf life, but must be refrigerated and served within a few days of opening. At 70 percent water, wet food will help keep your Chihuahua hydrated, but its rich consistency can also cause stomach upset and diarrhea as well as plaque and tartar buildup on teeth. Many veterinarians and breeders suggest a combination of wet and dry food for picky eaters. If your Chihuahua is a fussy eater, discuss combination options with your veterinarian or breeder.

Semi-moist: If dry food doesn't tempt your Chihuahua, and you (and your wallet) are not convinced that wet food is the best choice, semi-moist is a possible alternative. Semi-moist is soft to the bite, but still shaped into small, colorful pieces similar to dry food. It is a great choice for seniors with sensitive teeth and gums or for the picky eater that needs a little extra taste in his meals. Check the ingredient label before choosing a semi-moist food, as many of these products add extra corn syrup and preservatives for taste and shelf life. These extra ingredients can cause quick weight gain or stomach upset in your Chi.

WAYS TO ENCOURAGE THE FUSSY EATER

Not all Chihuahuas look forward to mealtimes, and keeping your Chihuahua at the proper weight is critical to his overall health. Chihuahuas are very active little dogs, and they can burn more calories per body-weight pound than normal-sized dogs. A dog's finicky eating habits may have to do with behavior and health. If you share fresh morsels of flank steak or salmon from your dinner plate with your Chihuahua, he may be holding off on his food to wait for a piece of yours. It's better to refrain from feeding table scraps to your tiny dog. If your dog stops eating his food completely, have your vet check him out to make sure nothing is amiss.

Here are some tips to coax the reluctant diner:

1. Offer your fussy pup his breakfast and dinner at the same time you eat your meals. This will make your Chihuahua feel like he's eating with his pack.

2. Select a premium brand of canned dog food made of real meat and vegetables. The better-quality wet foods smell like food, not preservatives—you can even recognize the peas and carrots!

3. Limit the number of treats you offer your Chihuahua. This tiny dog's caloric needs can be met by midday if you offer him a treat every hour.

4. Add some pizzazz to his regular food by adding some fresh cooked chicken or lean hamburger. Some Chis relish fresh green beans, chopped apples, and baby carrots. If you're offering dry food only, moisten the kibble with a half cup of low-salt chicken broth or a spoonful of a premium wet food.

For picky eaters, try a natural or home-cooked diet. Your Chihuahua may be sensitive to the preservatives that are often found in commercial food. Consult your vet on alternative feeding strategies.

What Not to Feed Your Chi

In addition to getting the balance correct, owners must also be aware that dogs cannot eat certain foods that their owners enjoy. Some foods disagree with dogs' systems, and others are actually toxic and can kill them—especially due to the Chihuahua's small size. According to the ASPCA, the following people foods should be avoided: chocolate, coffee, avocados, macadamia nuts, grapes, raisins, yeast dough, onions, garlic, and chives. Avoid milk because dogs lack sufficient amounts of the enzyme lactase in their systems; they cannot break down lactose in milk and milk products, often causing stomach upset and diarrhea.

5. Don't feed a fussy Chi from the table and don't share your snacks. Salty and sugary people food not only spoils the dog's appetite, it's actually bad for him (and you!).

6. Feed the dog in a quiet place, free of distractions, including visits from grabby toddlers or the nosy family cat.

7. Do not leave his food bowl on the floor for more than twenty minutes. The more feeding freedom you give to uninspired eaters, the pickier they become. A bowl of food sitting out for three hours says to the dog that he can eat whenever he wants, not at the appointed time. Like other crafty canines, Chihuahuas may pick at their food and wait for something tastier to come along in an hour or so.

8. Cancel the all-day buffet! Don't free-feed kibble. If your Chihuahua thinks he's lives at an all-you-can-eat smorgasbord, he'll eventually get bored and not look forward to mealtimes.

SLIMMING DOWN THE CHOWHOUND

Some Chihuahuas have a tendency to overindulge at mealtimes, and excessive weight on a dog this small can lead to health problems that will shorten his life. Dog owners, the cookie-offering culprits in question, are generally fast to defend their plump kids, but if you can't see your Chihuahua's waist (ribs barely visible with a slight ripple over them) and your friends are calling him Chunky Monkey, it may be time for a reality check and a veterinary checkup. It takes surprisingly little food to keep a normal, active Chihuahua in good health.

Here's some friendly advice to help get your Chi on the road to a healthy weight:

1. Count calories. A full-grown, active Chihuahua requires less food per pound of body weight per day than you might expect.

2. Purchase low-calorie varieties of dog foods and treats.

3. Eliminate dog treats from his diet. Instead offer little pieces of apple or banana.

4. New house rule: no table scraps. Make sure every member of the family knows the rule and obeys it, including the kids who let the dog eat their sandwich crusts and grandpa who's tossing him bits of his pizza while watching *Jeopardy!*

Over-feeding the Chihuahua can lead to obesity, which can be accompanied by abnormal bone development, such as bone weakening and leg bowing, skin problems, and rickets. When in doubt, it is better to stick to a lean diet. Lean dogs live longer, healthier, more energetic lives. Take the time to research and plan your dog's diet, and ask your veterinarian any and all questions that may come to mind about your Chihuahua's nutrition. Feeding is an important aspect of dog ownership that can't (and shouldn't) be overlooked—a healthy diet is the key to a lasting, meaningful life with your Chihuahua.

At a Glance ...

Ask your breeder or veterinarian to help you understand dog-food ingredients and nutrition labels. Depending on your dog's age, weight, and lifestyle, he may need an assortment of different protein and vitamin combinations to fulfill his daily needs.

Consider your dog's likes, dislikes, and health requirements when choosing dog food. There are several different lifestage formulas—puppy, adult, and senior—in several different types—dry, wet, and semi-moist—to choose from. When in doubt, consult your veterinarian.

Are you raising a picky eater? Is your dog allergic or sensitive to common ingredients found in store-bought dog food? Alternative diets, such as all-natural products or cooking for your dog at home may be the key to your Chihuahua's dietary needs. Take the time to research these alternative feeding plans before switching your Chihuahua to a home-cooked or natural diet.

CHAPTER NINE

Small and Stunning

With a dog as small as the Chihuahua, regardless of coat length, the task of grooming will not be time-consuming, but it is just as important as it is for any other dog. If you introduce your dog to grooming when he's just a puppy, he'll take a liking to it because Chis love to spend time with their people and enjoy being the center of attention.

Whether your Chihuahua has a long or smooth coat, it's best to brush your dog on a

Because Chihuahuas are indoors for most of the day, your dog will only need a bath once every four to six weeks. Brush him daily to keep his skin and fur in top condition.

grooming table or on a firm table with a nonslip surface. You will find that many Chihuahua owners use slightly different pieces of equipment, depending on what works best for them. Ask your breeder for advice on grooming tools and techniques. In time, you'll discover what your dog enjoys and the best way to accomplish the various grooming tasks required to keep your dog looking his best.

YOUR CHIHUAHUA'S COAT

Regular brushing with a soft-bristle brush will keep your Chihuahua's coat clean and shiny. It's not necessary to bathe your dog frequently, but brushing your Chi every day is a good idea because brushing will remove any loose hair from the long or smooth coat. The long-coated Chihuahua isn't particularly prone to tangling, matting, or knotting, so grooming is almost as easy as it is for the smooth-coated Chi. Just run a steel-toothed comb through the long-coat's hair to

prevent tangling. It is always wise to check your dog daily for bumps, parasites, or any other unexpected problems as they may be symptoms of a larger medical issue. Talk to your veterinarian about any unexpected changes in your Chihuahua's body or coat.

In addition to a soft-bristle brush and a steel-toothed comb, some owners like to use a small rubber curry comb to help massage and stimulate the Chihuahua's skin. Massaging with a curry comb in the direction of the coat's growth also helps keep the coat glossy. Your Chihuahua will enjoy this doggy-spa moment with you! You can also use a chamois or piece of velvet for the finishing touches on the smooth coat (or look for a two-sided grooming mitt, with soft leather on one side and velvet on the other), which will remove dust and loose hair.

BATH TIME!

Most owners opt to bathe their Chihuahuas monthly, perhaps more often for long-coated Chihuahuas. Show dogs are usually bathed before each show, but pets can squeak by with a bath every six weeks or so, depending on the dog, the time of year, and the dog's environment. The kitchen or bathroom sink is the ideal location for bathing your tiny Chihuahua. The bathtub is too big and overwhelming for the Chihuahua, so some owners place a small basin in the bathtub to make the Chihuahua feel more secure.

Regardless of the location you choose, make sure to place your Chihuahua on a nonslip surface while in the bath. If a Chihuahua puppy is introduced to the bath at ten to twelve weeks of age, he will accept bathing as a part of the normal grooming routine as he grows older. Make bath time a positive experience for

Did You Know?

With a dog as long-lived as the Chihuahua, pet insurance can pay off many times over. There are a number of options available to owners, offering various plans at affordable prices. Visit the AKC website (www.akc.org) to learn more about the AKC Pet Healthcare Plan available through Pet Partners®.

the dog. Shower him with lots of praise and treats before showering him with the wet stuff!

Before placing your Chihuahua in the bath, brush the dog's coat out thoroughly. Fill the basin or sink with a few inches of warm water and then place the dog on the rubber mat or whatever nonslip surface you've chosen. Select a good-quality dog shampoo; human products are too harsh and will dry out your dog's skin. Fill a bucket or another basin with clean water so you can use it to rinse the puppy after you've finished applying the shampoo. You can either pour the clean water over the dog after you've drained the sink, or you can place the dog into the clean basin to remove the soap. When running additional water into the bath, be sure that the temperature isn't too hot or too cold (test it on the back of your hand first). Be sure to shampoo the dog's whole body, including his under parts, tail, and feet. Wash the dog's face and head last, and take extra care to avoid getting water and soap in the dog's eyes and ears. Most dogs don't like to have their heads wet, so wait until the end of the bath; this also helps avoid dripping shampoo into the dog's eyes while you're working on another part of his body.

Be sure to rinse all the soap out of the dog's coat. Soap left in the dog's coat can cause skin irritation later. After you finish rinsing the soap out of the coat, lift your dog from the bath and wrap him in a clean, warm towel. Use a blow-dryer set on the lowest setting to dry your Chihuahua. Take the time to introduce your Chihuahua to the sound and feel of the blow-dryer so that he is comfortable with it before using it for the first time. Dogs do not like water or air in their face, so take care not to allow the air to blow directly into your Chihuahua's face. Keep him indoors, away from drafts and out of mischief, until his coat is completely dry.

EARS AND EYES

Being so close to the floor, the Chihuahua's ears and eyes are particularly prone to dust and debris, so wipe your dog's face and ears clean every day. He'll appreciate the daily facial. Pet stores sell special formulas for cleaning dogs' ears and eyes.

Chihuahuas also can be prone to tear stains, and left unattended these stains can be very difficult to remove. Purchase a cleansing product made specifically for tear stains, and gently apply it with a cotton ball. You can minimize tear stains by applying a little protective petroleum jelly under each eye, which will also protect the dog's skin.

Begin grooming your Chi as soon as you bring him home from the breeder. He will quickly get used to the routine and will enjoy this special time with his favorite human—you!

Be wary of any sign of injury to the eyes, and if found, seek veterinary attention immediately. If an eye injury is dealt with quickly, it can often be repaired; if neglected, it can lead to loss of vision.

The smooth coat's ears can get a little greasy, and wiping them frequently helps. It's not uncommon for smooth Chihuahuas to lose hair in their ears, leaving the skin leathers bare, which can promote extra grease and skin oils to form. An anti-bacterial soap can remedy the greasy-ear situation. Once the greasiness subsides, brush the ear with a very soft baby brush until the hair grows back.

If your dog has been shaking his head or scratching at his ears, he may well have an ear-mite infestation or an infection of some kind. A thick brown discharge and bad smell may also indicate these problems; if your Chihuahua shows any of these symptoms, veterinary consultation is needed right away.

NAILS AND FEET

Your Chihuahua's nails must always be trimmed, but how frequently they need clipping depends on the surface upon which your dog walks. Chis living primarily on carpets or grass will need more frequent nail clipping than those who regularly walk on cement or blacktop.

Your Chi should be trained to accept nail clipping from an early age. Take great care not to cut the quick, the blood vessel that runs through the nail, as this is painful—much like when you cut your own nails too short. It is a good idea to keep a styptic pencil or some styptic powder on hand to stop the bleeding in case of an accident. Cutting just a small tip of nail at a time is the safest approach. You

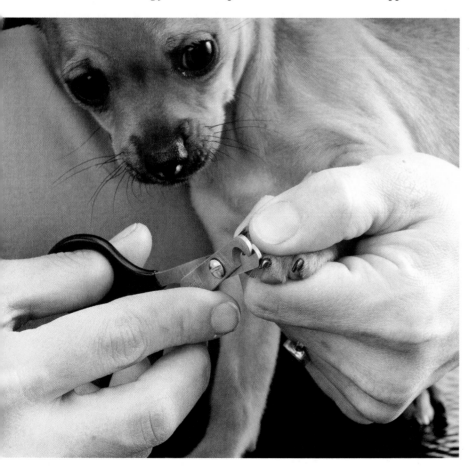

Good Housekeeping

Chihuahuas are generally very clean dogs. They don't shed too much, and they're quite fastidious in their habits. The dog's cleanliness is an advantage to owners, but due to the Chi's small size and close proximity to flooring, carpets, tile, and so forth, the dog is more susceptible to dust, dirt, and debris than other dogs. In fact, a dust bunny on your floor is more like a dust pony to the Chihuahua! Owners of tiny dogs must vacuum and mop frequently to help keep their Chihuahua's environment as clean and safe as possible.

When trimming your Chi's nails, use a scissor- or guillotine-style nail-clipping tool made especially for dogs. Using human nail-clippers can damage or splinter your Chihuahua's sensitive nails.

should also inspect your Chi's feet regularly to be sure that nothing has become wedged or embedded between the pads.

TEETH

Don't forget to brush your Chihuahua's pearly whites. According to the American Veterinary Dental Society, 80 percent of dogs show signs of oral disease as early as age three. Further studies prove that good oral hygiene can add three to five years to a dog's life. Signs of periodontal disease include bad breath, red, inflamed gums, and yellow and brown tartar buildup along the gum line. You should brush your dog's teeth at least twice a week using a dog toothbrush and dog toothpaste. Don't use human toothpaste as it can be harmful to your dog. Start this grooming habit early, and your dog will quickly get used to having a toothbrush in his mouth. He'll most likely even come to enjoy the liver- or chicken-flavored toothpaste that you can purchase at your local pet store.

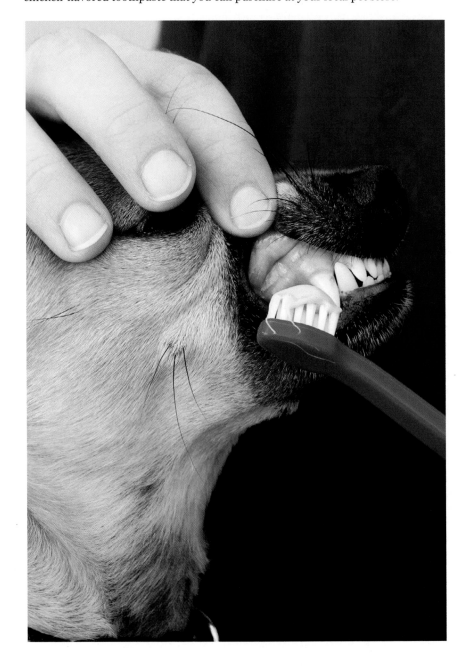

Brushing a dog's teeth is a chore often overlooked by dog owners, but neglected teeth and gums can quickly lead to more serious health problems such as oral infection and liver and kidney disease.

Grooming Supplies

Here are the items you will need to groom your Chihuahua:

BATHING

☐ A handheld spray attachment for your tub or sink

☐ A rubber mat for the dog to stand on

☐ A tearless dog shampoo and conditioner (don't use human products)

☐ Towels (a chamois is best)

☐ A pet hair dryer (you can use your own, but set it on low and cool)

☐ Spritz-on dry shampoo (handy in case you need a quick cleanup to get rid of dirt or odor)

BRUSHING COAT

☐ Soft-bristle brush or rubber curry comb

☐ Stainless-steel comb

TRIMMING NAILS

☐ Dog nail cutters (scissor- or guillotine-type)

☐ Nail file or grinder

☐ Styptic pencil or styptic powder (in case you cut the quick)

BRUSHING TEETH

☐ Dog toothbrush or rough washcloth

☐ Dog toothpaste (don't use human toothpaste)

CLEANING EARS AND EYES

☐ A soft baby brush

☐ Cotton balls or wipes

☐ Liquid ear-cleaning solution

☐ Tear stain cleaner

☐ Dog eye wipes

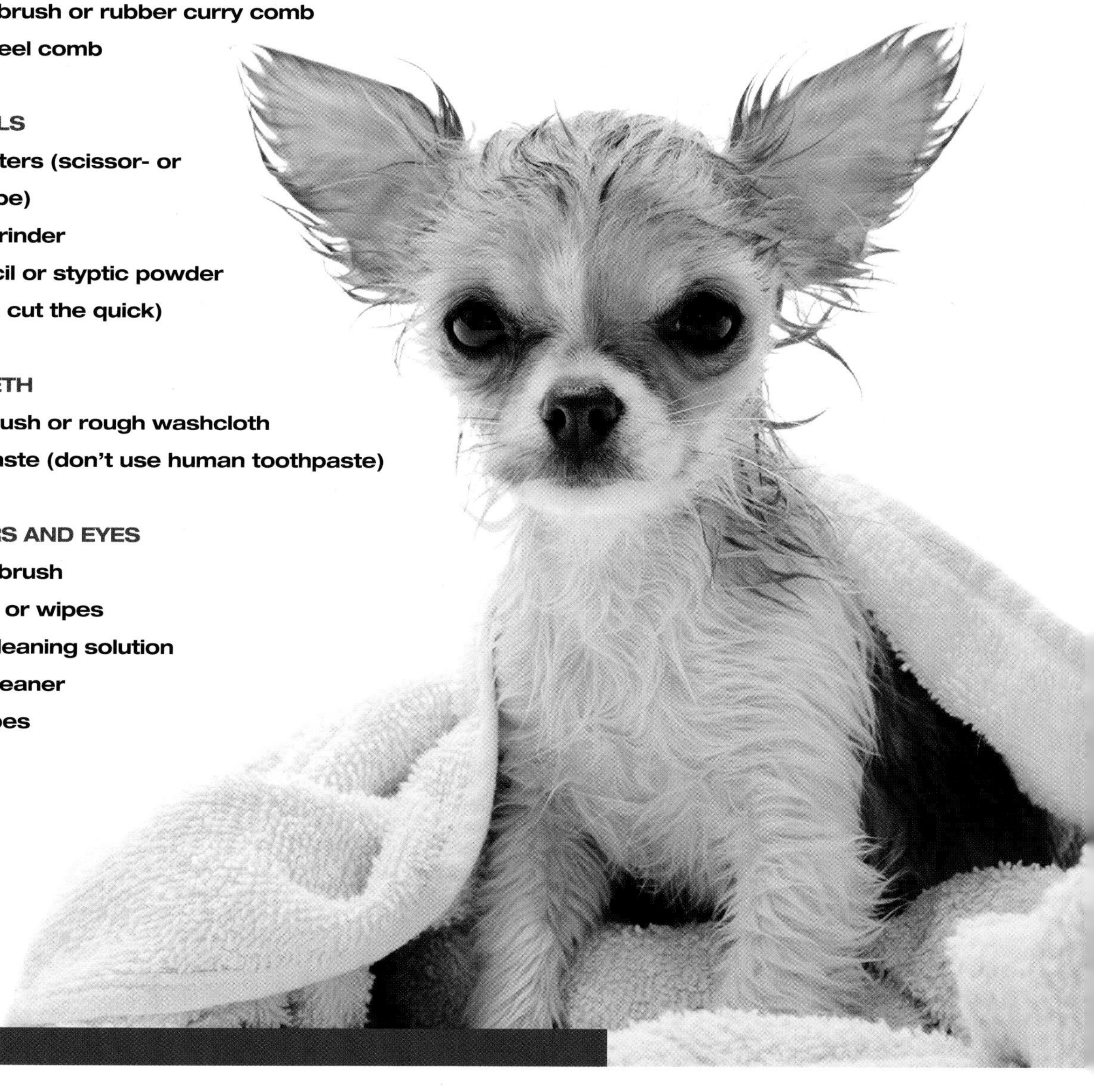

PROFESSIONAL GROOMERS

If you prefer to bring your Chihuahua to a salon instead of grooming and bathing him at home, be sure to select a professional groomer whom you can trust. Choosing a grooming salon is a lot like finding a hair salon for yourself. Look for both skill and personality. Don't be afraid to ask the groomer about his or her experience in grooming. Larger pet shops and pet superstores may also offer grooming services.

Has the groomer attended grooming school? Is he or she a master groomer? Many groomers belong to national associations, and membership in such organizations speaks well of the groomer's interest in professional standards and staying current on safety as well as new equipment, styles, and other trends. Three examples of national associations are the National Dog Groomers Association of America (www.nationaldoggroomers.com), the International Society of Canine Cosmetologists (www.petstylist.com), and International Professional Groomers, Inc. (www.ipgicmg.com). If you intend to have your dog treated for fleas and ticks, some states require a certification; however, no state requires a license for grooming, so you must be careful when selecting a groomer.

Safety First

Grooming should be a fun, relaxing time for your Chihuahua, so play it smart and safe. Experience is the best teacher, but here are a few reminders:

- **Never leave a dog unattended in the bath tub.**
- **Never leave a dog attached to a noose on a grooming table, and never walk away from a dog standing on any table.**
- **Handle the Chihuahua carefully when he comes out of the bath; Chihuahuas are "slippery when wet."**
- **Never plunge the dog into a basin of water before you test the temperature; the water should be a moderate, warm temperature that would be comfortable for you.**
- **Protect the dog's ears during baths (a small piece of cotton in each ear can prevent water getting into the ears, but be sure you remember to remove the cotton after the bath).**
- **Purchase the best-quality grooming tools and dog shampoo you can afford; it's always better (and most cost-effective in the end) to buy the best products in the beginning rather than opting for inferior supplies that will need to be replaced multiple times.**
- **Keep sharp objects away from your Chihuahua; purchase round-edged scissors instead of pointed, sharp ones.**
- **Have a styptic pencil or powder on hand in case you accidently clip the quick in the dog's nail.**

When visiting a groomer, make sure that the salon is clean and organized, with a knowledgeable staff. Credentials from a certification program of some sort should be displayed prominently on a wall, which assures customers that the groomer is aware of current safety and hygiene practices, how to handle pesticides, and how to work with dogs of all breeds and sizes. Avoid any groomer who wishes to anesthetize your dog for a grooming procedure.

Introduce your Chi to the groomer and observe the groomer's rapport with the dog. The groomer should ask if your dog has special needs or if you have any concerns. If you're aware of any allergies or sensitivities, be sure to let the groomer know. The groomer will be grateful that you've trained your Chi to stand politely on a table and that you've exposed the dog to a bath or two at home as well as the sound and feel of a blow-dryer. Be sure to ask about the drying method used at the salon. It's best not to allow your dog to be placed in a drying cage (which is similar to a crate with fans embedded into its sides), which are often set too high and too hot for the tiny Chihuahua to handle. Make sure your Chi is up-to-date on all his vaccinations before bringing him to the groomer (or any public place where other dogs will be). Some shops require this, but for the safety of your Chi, rabies and Bordetella shots must be current.

Always trust your gut instinct when selecting a professional service provider, whether it's a groomer, trainer, petsitter, or veterinarian. If you don't feel comfortable leaving your Chihuahua, don't! Remember, too, that Chihuahuas are extremely sensitive, which means they will pick up on their owners' emotions and become fearful and unhappy. When dropping off your Chihuahua at the groomer, be sure to keep an upbeat and confident attitude. In time, and with the right groomer, your Chihuahua should be happy to visit the salon each month.

A flea comb can help discover the presence of fleas or ticks in your Chi's coat. If your Chihuahua has a case of the itchies, run a comb through his hair to investigate.

At a Glance ...

Your Chihuahua's coat is easy to care for. However, because he is so close to the ground, your Chi will pick up an assortment of dust and debris in his coat, eyes, and ears. Brush through your Chihuahua's coat once a day to keep him glistening and clean.

. . . .

Long-coated Chihuahuas require a little extra grooming than short coats. The long, wavy fur needs daily brushing to keep it tangle-free and fluffy.

. . . .

Start grooming your Chihuahua while he is a young puppy. This includes brushing, bathing, and cleaning his eyes, ears, and teeth. If you familiarize your Chi puppy with a grooming ritual, he will quickly get used to the process and even come to enjoy the one-on-one time with you!

. . . .

Finding a responsible groomer is no easy task. Ask for recommendations from your breeder and veterinarian, and visit the groomer before dropping your Chihuahua off for the day. Ask questions about the groomer's history and grooming process. You want to be sure you are comfortable with the groomer and his or her techniques before you trust the salon with your Chihuahua.

CHAPTER TEN

Staying Fit and Healthy

Owning a Chihuahua requires twice the commitment of any other dog. Keep this in mind, as well as the fact that Chis can outlive most dogs two to one! With proper health care and high-quality food, a well-bred Chihuahua can enjoy a life expectancy of nearly twenty years. While that may be a fraction of a human's lifetime, it's many years longer than most other dog breeds. The general rule of thumb with dogs is the smaller the breed, the

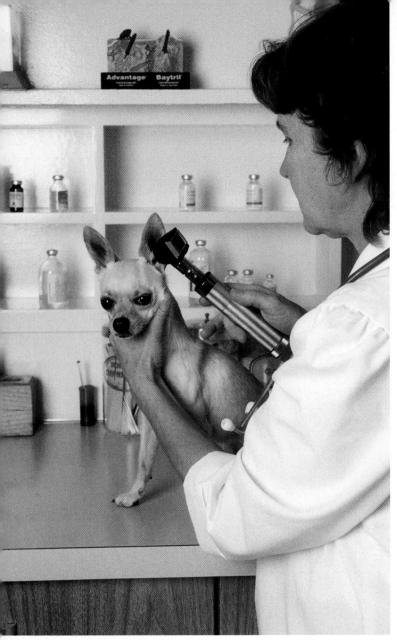

At your Chihuahua's yearly check-ups, the veterinarian will give your dog a full physical, checking his eyes, ears, heart, lungs, and overall body structure. The vet will also check your Chi for any parasites.

longer it lives—though there are happy exceptions to every rule.

Knowing that your Chihuahua could reach the two-decade mark adds significant responsibility to the owner's role and underscores the need for exceptional health care. A healthy dog's quality of life begins and ends with his veterinarian. Choose your vet carefully, considering all of the factors, not simply location and costs. Visit the AKC website (www.akc .org) for a complete list of veterinary practices that participate in the AKC Veterinary Network Program.

CHOOSING A GOOD VETERINARIAN

Finding a qualified veterinarian close to your home is no easy task. Ask for recommendations from your breeder, other pet owners in your neighborhood, and your local breed club. Do your vet research before you bring home your Chihuahua puppy from the breeder. That way, you can schedule an initial checkup within a couple of days of your puppy's homecoming. Here are a few things to keep in mind when searching for a veterinarian:

• **Location:** If possible, select a veterinarian whose practice is within fifteen to twenty minutes from your home. Is the clinic in a busy part of town or on a heavy-traffic road? Is there parking?

• **Experience:** Specific knowledge of Toy dogs is an important qualification. If you live in a rural area, be sure that you choose a vet who has plenty of experience with companion animals. Many rural vets are comfortable with horses and farm animals, but have limited experience with dogs (especially Toy breeds).

• **Reputation:** Ask your breeder as well as dog-owning friends and neighbors for veterinarian references. Contact your state's veterinary medical board to confirm your chosen vet's certification as well as reputation. Is the clinic certified with the American Animal Hospital Association (AAHA)? Have there ever been any complaints filed?

• **Personality:** Spend time talking to the vet and get a sense of what he or she is like. Do you get a good feeling about his or her sincerity, table-side manner, and communication skills?

• **Outlook:** Most veterinarians practice preventive conventional medicine, but if you're interested in a combination of conventional and holistic methods, such as acupuncture, homeopathy, herbs, and massage, you'll have to find a vet who practices an integrative approach.

• **Facility and staff:** Is the practice clean and modern? Is it busy? Are the office hours convenient? How long does it typically take to get an appointment?

Are the vet techs and other staff members knowledgeable, accommodating, and friendly? Do they like small dogs?

- **Payment:** Is the schedule of fees for services clearly posted or stated in print? Does the practice accept your pet insurance? Which methods of payment are acceptable? Which credit cards? How is billing done?

- **Other services:** Does the practice offer boarding or grooming services? Does the office administer microchips? Does it offer emergency care and, if so, is the facility staffed overnight? If the vet does not offer emergency services, is it associated with a 24-hour veterinary clinic? Are any of the vets in the practice specialists in other areas, such as dermatology, cardiology, or hematology? Are diagnostic tests such as X-rays, EKGs, and blood work done in the office?

BE A GOOD CLIENT

You've heard it said that your veterinarian is your dog's second best friend, but relationships are always a two-way street. The rapport you establish with your veterinarian is dependent on the vet's personality and experience as well as on your own behavior. Observe the following pointers to become your vet's favorite client and a better doggy parent:

- Be considerate and patient. Make appointments and keep them. Realize that you aren't the veterinarian's only client.

- Train your dog so that he's mannerly and under control at the vet's office. The more well-behaved your Chi acts at the office, the better able the veterinarian

Due to their small size, Chihuahuas may be extra sensitive to vaccinations and other medications. Talk to your vet about the appropriate vaccines and dosages beforehand.

CORE Vaccines
Check with your vet, but all puppies should receive vaccines for the following diseases:

CONDITION	TREATMENT	PROGNOSIS	VACCINE NEEDED
ADENOVIRUS-2 (immunizes against Adenovirus-1, the agent of infectious canine hepatitis)	No curative therapy for infectious hepatitis; treatment geared toward minimizing neurologic effects, shock, hemorrhage, secondary infections	Self-limiting but cross-protects against infectious hepatitis, which is highly contagious and can be mild to rapidly fatal	Recommended
DISTEMPER	No specific treatment; supportive treatment (IV fluids, antibiotics)	High mortality rates	Highly recommended
PARVOVIRUS-2	No specific treatment; supportive treatment (IV fluids, antibiotics)	Highly contagious to young puppies; high mortality rates	Highly recommended
RABIES	No treatment	Fatal	Required

will be able to assess his condition. It's difficult for a vet to properly diagnose a Chi who is fearful and nervous in the examination room.

- Always transport your Chi to the clinic in his pet carrier.

- Listen attentively to the vet, take notes when he or she makes recommendations, and follow up on the advice you receive.

- Bring your Chi to the vet regularly, once or twice a year for annual checkups, not only when you have a health concern.

- Know your Chi's signs of wellness and look out for symptoms of ill health, such as a dull coat, parasites, loose stool, drooling, eye watering, and so forth.

- Observe your dog's behavior at home and note any unusual behavior or change in his routine (eating and bathroom habits, sensitivities, listlessness).

- Before driving to the veterinarian's office with an emergency, call to give the office staff advance notice so that they can be prepared for your arrival.

- Know when to fold: if you discover that your veterinarian and you don't see eye to eye, find another vet.

Traveling to the veterinarian's office with a Chihuahua should be very simple, especially if you've crate-trained your dog. A crate is not only the most convenient way to transport your Chihuahua but also the safest. It's best to protect your Chi from the unwanted attention of large or aggressive dogs, for he may be feeling a little off-color and appreciate a little peace and quiet.

Health Alert

The Chihuahua Club of America recommends testing dogs for patella luxation, eye diseases, heart conditions, and possibly syringomyelia and canine brucellosis. Syringomyelia (SM), also known as "neck scratcher's disease," is a very serious brain and spinal cord disease, only identified by MRI. Canine brucellosis is an infectious disease that affects the reproductive system, possibly causing abortions and infertility as well as problems with the backbone, eyes, kidneys, brain, and lymph nodes. Canine brucellosis is spread via bacterium during breeding and is transmissible to other dogs and humans. Puppy buyers should inquire whether or not breeders have tested their sires and dams prior to breeding.

Smile Pretty!

Your Chihuahua's dental health is your responsibility. Keep in mind that unhealthy teeth and gums affect more than your dog's mouth. Dental problems aren't just missing teeth and bad breath. When gums are infected with gingivitis or periodontitis, all sorts of other health problems can subsequently arise, spreading through the dog's major organs and possibly shortening his life. Due to their tiny mouths and teeth, Toy dogs are prone to dental problems, so Chihuahua owners should take dental issues and grooming habits very seriously.

VACCINATIONS

Your puppy should have received his first vaccinations when he was five or six weeks old while still with the breeder. Upon purchasing your puppy, your breeder should have provided you with a list of vaccinations your Chihuahua received and tests he completed while in the breeder's care. Take these health records to your first veterinary appointment.

Your veterinarian will talk to you about which vaccinations your puppy still requires and will set up a schedule for the remainder of his shots. Although vaccination protocols differ among veterinarians and in different regions of the country, most vets recommend a series of "combination" shots given every three to four weeks. Combinations shots include multiple vaccines in each injection. Some breeders and veterinarians feel that some combination shots are too strong for a dog as small as the Chihuahua, so discuss the alternative possibility of giving your puppy a series of individual vaccination injections instead.

Depending on where you live, the recommended vaccinations will vary, and veterinarians have their own opinions on which vaccinations are necessary. Often you'll hear of assorted vaccines referred to as "core" and "non-core." The American Veterinary Medical Association (AVMA) recommends a series of core vaccines that are encouraged for all dogs throughout the country. Major core vaccines include adenovirus, distemper, parvovirus, and rabies, all of which are highly recommended and/or required by law in most states. Non-core vaccines are highly recommended for dogs that live in certain areas of the country, depending on the regional threats in the dog's environment. Some of these diseases include canine parainfluenza, leptospirosis, coronavirus, Bordetella (kennel cough), and Lyme disease (borreliosis). Your veterinarian will let you know of the diseases common in your region of the country and recommend which vaccinations are necessary for your Chihuahua.

Visit the American Animal Hospital Association's website at www.aahanet .org/Library/CanineVaccine.aspx for a detailed report on common core and non-core vaccines recommended for your puppy. The AVMA also has a helpful webpage about pet vaccinations at www.avma.org/issues/vaccination.

Your veterinarian will set up a suitable vaccination schedule to complete the necessary puppy shots and inform you when booster shots are due. When you

Other Vaccines and Treatment

Depending on where you live and your dog's needs, the following ailments and diseases can be treated through your veterinarian:

CONDITION	TREATMENT	PROGNOSIS	RECOMMENDATION
BORDETELLA (KENNEL COUGH)	Keep warm; humidify room; moderate exercise	Highly contagious; rarely fatal in healthy dogs; easily treated	Optional vaccine; prevalence varies; vaccine may be linked to acute reactions; low efficacy
FLEA AND TICK INFESTATION	Topical and ingestible	Highly contagious	Preventive treatment highly recommended
HEARTWORM	Arsenical compound; rest; restricted exercise	Widely occurring infections; preventive programs available regionally; successful treatment after early detection	Preventive treatment highly recommended
INTESTINAL WORMS	Dewormer; home medication regimen	Good with prompt treatment	Preventive treatment highly recommended
LYME DISEASE (BORRELIOSIS)	Antibiotics	Can't completely eliminate the organism, but can be controlled in most cases	Vaccine recommended only for dogs with high risk of exposure to deer ticks
PARAINFLUENZA	Rest; humidify room; moderate exercise	Highly contagious; mild; self-limiting; rarely fatal	Vaccine optional but recommended; doesn't block infection, but lessens clinical signs
PERIODONTITIS	Dental cleaning; extractions; repair	Excellent, but involves anesthesia	Preventive treatment recommended

Cool Down

If you notice your Chihuahua panting, drooling, or exhibiting increased body temperature, reddened gums, rapid heart rate, irregular heartbeats, and/or dehydration, heatstroke (or hyperthermia) may be underway. Apply cold water immediately, especially over the shoulders. In severe cases, the dog should be submerged in cool water (not icy) up to his neck. Dogs can die quickly from heatstroke, so urgent veterinary attention is of paramount importance. A dog's normal body temperature is 101 to 102.5 degrees Fahrenheit, and hyperthermia is indicated between 103 and 106 degrees.

visit your vet for the puppy's first shots, be extra careful not to let your Chihuahua come into close contact with other dogs in the waiting room. Visits to the vet should be to stay well. At this first visit, the vet will examine your new puppy, checking his heart, lungs, and overall condition. Bring along a stool sample so that the vet can check for internal parasites.

CHECKING FOR PARASITES

Fleas and ticks can really bug your Chihuahua! Infestations are no laughing matter, and owners must be proactive in preventing the onset of parasites in their dogs' coats. The sight of a single flea on your Chihuahua's coat indicates that you

Support Canine Health Research

The mission of the American Kennel Club Canine Health Foundation, Inc. (AKC CHF) is to advance the health of all dogs by funding sound scientific research and supporting the dissemination of health information to prevent, treat, and cure canine disease. The foundation makes grants to fund a variety of health efforts:

- Identifying the cause(s) of disease
- Earlier, more accurate diagnosis
- Developing screening tests for breeders
- Accurate, positive prognosis
- Effective, efficient treatment

The AKC CHF also supports educational programs that bring scientists together to discuss their work and develop new collaborations to further advance canine health.

The AKC created the foundation in 1995 to raise funds to support canine health research. Each year the AKC CHF allocates $1.5 million to new health-research projects.

How You Can Help: If you have an AKC-registered dog, submit his DNA sample (cheek swab or blood sample) to the Canine Health Information Center (CHIC) DNA databank (www.caninehealthinfo.org). Encourage regular health testing by breeders, get involved with your local dog club, and support the efforts to host health education programs. And, if possible, make a donation.

For information, contact the AKC Canine Health Foundation, P.O. Box 900061, Raleigh, NC 27675-9061 or check out the website at www.akcchf.org.

have a problem. Fleas travel in groups! Ask your veterinarian about preventive aids for fleas, which often come in liquid or pill form. Some dogs have sensitivity to flea remedies, so proceed with caution and always with the guidance of a professional. If your Chihuahua has access to your lawn, be sure that the grass is treated with a dog-safe product during the mild months to kill fleas and ticks on your property.

If you are faced with a flea infestation, you must treat the dog as well as his whole environment, indoors and out. In addition to the medications provided by your vet, a good grooming salon should be able to "dip" the dog to kill any adult fleas on his body. Indoors you'll have to "bomb" the house with an insecticide preparation to kill adult fleas and use an insect-growth-regulator spray to kill the immature forms of eggs, larvae, and pupae. Prior to treating the house, vacuum all carpets, furniture, and bedding around the house and then promptly discard

Choose a veterinarian for your Chihuahua's lifetime. A vet that has treated your dog yearly since puppyhood will be more knowledgeable of your Chi's health-care history as he ages.

A PIECE OF HISTORY

Before the late 1800s, rabies was considered a deadly and incurable disease. If a dog or human was infected with the neurological virus, they would die within a matter of days. In 1885, two French scientists, Louis Pasteur and Émile Roux, developed a rabies vaccination by injecting weakened and/or dead samples of the virus into affected (and unaffected) individuals so that their immune systems would naturally create an immunity to the disease. Today, a modern rabies vaccination is required for all dogs and cats in all fifty states.

the vacuum bag. To be completely thorough, contact an exterminator or land-scaper to treat your lawn as well.

Ticks are a problem for dogs and humans who live close to wooded areas, though the prominence of ticks in other areas has been rising in recent years. The deer tick transmits Lyme disease (borreliosis), which is contagious to humans and is frequently misdiagnosed; Dermacentor ticks spread Rocky Mountain spotted fever as well as Colorado tick fever; and the brown dog tick spreads ehrlichiosis. Discuss tick protection with your veterinarian, as there may be a few extra vaccines your dog should have if you live in tick-prone areas.

Always be on the lookout for signs of ear mites infesting your little dog's big ears. Mites cannot be seen by the naked eye, but if you notice a smelly, brown discharge in your dog's ears, and he is shaking his head or scratching at his ears, you can bet that mites are present. Your vet can prescribe a preparation to remedy the itchy situation.

A dog can also carry internal parasites in the form of worms. Ascarid roundworms are the most common, but tapeworms, although less frequent, can be even more debilitating. Most puppies are born with roundworm larvae in their systems, and most breeders will deworm their puppies at least twice before sending them to their permanent homes. However, be sure to take a close look at your puppy's droppings, as tapeworms and roundworms can be seen with the naked eye—tapeworm segments look like moving grains of rice, and roundworms look like strands of cooked spaghetti.

Heartworms are transmitted by mosquitoes and are very dangerous for all dogs. They gather in your dog's heart and are often fatal if not caught early enough. Watch for symptoms of possible worm infestation in your Chihuahua: distended belly, vomiting, diarrhea, trouble going to the bathroom, dry hair, and rapid weight loss. Routine worming is essential throughout a dog's life and a suitable preventive regimen prescribed by a veterinarian is certainly advised.

NEUTERING AND SPAYING

Will spaying or neutering change your Chihuahua's sweet and loving personality? Absolutely not! The advantages of spaying and neutering far outweigh the possible health concerns that face unaltered dogs. Some Chihuahuas are sensitive to anesthesia so be sure to discuss the risks with your veterinarian prior to scheduling a surgery.

The AKC advises all dog owners, "Unless you know you are going to show your dog, it is best to have your female spayed and your male neutered." Both operations are extremely safe and benefit the dog's long-term health. A spayed female will be less prone to uterine infections and mammary cancer, and a neutered male will be less at risk for testicular cancer. Likewise, spayed female Chihuahuas will not cycle twice or thrice annually, and males are less likely to roam in search of a female and will less aggressively defend their home and property.

As your Chihuahua ages, make a few changes around the house. Provide ramps and steps to help your Chi onto the couch and shorten your daily walks. Your elderly Chi will be very appreciative.

AGING CHIHUAHUAS

If you provide your Chihuahua with a sensible, nutritious diet, ample exercise, and good veterinary care, you should be fortunate to see your dog live into his double digits. Once he is ten years of age, begin taking him to the veterinarian at least twice a year for a basic health checkup. Your vet will take yearly blood work to check for liver and kidney function and check for heart murmurs, hearing loss, cataracts, and other age-related conditions that can be prevented and treated to keep your Chihuahua happy and comfortable in his elder years.

Chihuahuas can stay active well into their teens, although owners should shorten their daily walks and limit the amount of outdoor time on hot summer days and in the cold winter. Seniors will require more frequent potty trips and may have the occasional house-training accident. This is the time for patience, not correction. Arthritis affects many senior dogs, so be sure to offer your Chi a soft bed away from drafts. As the dog's vision and hearing begin to diminish, your Chihuahua may become less interested in play and socialization, startle more easily, and act more irritably. Keep children and other dogs away from a senior that's not feeling at his perky best. Senior dogs, like older people, have good days and bad. Make the most of your Chi's good days and give him lots of love and affection to let him know that he's still your number-one boy.

Your Chihuahua is completely dependent on you. With good grooming, daily exercise, preventive health care, and a nutritious diet, your Chihuahua should live a long, happy, and energetic life. Your Chihuahua will be your best friend and loyal charge for a lifetime.

Preventive health care is more than just yearly visits to the veterinarian. Keep an eye on your Chi's daily habits and body as he ages. Write down any questions or concerns you have to ask at your next vet visit.

At a Glance ...

The best form of health care is a preventive strategy. Take your Chihuahua to the veterinarian at least once a year (twice if he's a senior) for a basic wellness checkup. Your vet should be able to catch any health problems early and treat them effectively.

· ·

Vaccinations and booster shots are an important part of puppy care as well as ongoing adult health maintenance. Depending on where you live, your veterinarian will recommend specific vaccinations for your Chihuahua. Do your research, and keep up on your annual veterinary visits and vaccination schedules.

· ·

Most dogs fall victim to some sort of parasite in their lifetime. Be on the lookout for symptoms of fleas and ticks (itching, scratching, and flaky brown dirt in the coat) and worms (vomiting, diarrhea, and weight loss). Your vet will prescribe the right medication to help protect your pup from pesky pests!

CHAPTER ELEVEN

Activities for You and Your Chi

The Chihuahua loves to be busy! A clan of happy Chihuahuas is in perpetual motion, a blur of fur and festivity. These little dogs can motor about their homes and yards to get all the exercise they need and desire. The breed's quick metabolism keeps the Chihuahua burning calories at a rate faster than most other dogs, proportionally pound for pound. But, your Chihuahua still needs a daily exercise regimen to keep him both physically and mentally fit.

Bored with your daily walk around the neighborhood? Take your Chihuahua to a local dog park or for a short romp at the beach. Your Chi will love the exercise and the excitement of visiting a new place.

If you are lucky enough (and smart enough!) to have more than one Chihuahua, your Chi gang will provide each other with constant exercise and entertainment. If yours is an only pet, you must become his playmate and workout partner. Introduce your Chihuahua to a structured schedule of exercise and play. Dogs love to spend time with their owners, and outdoor activity time will definitely be the highlight of your Chi's day. Despite the breed's active nature, don't expect your Chihuahua to keep pace with you while you're out on a brisk morning run or a late afternoon bicycle ride. The Chi wasn't built for that, and his four-inch legs cannot last miles on end. The Chihuahua enjoys moderate exercise, including a walk around the block or a game of fetch in the backyard. When exercising your Chihuahua, be sensible:

• Limit play sessions to fifteen or twenty minutes. Get to know your dog and his limitations.

• Gradually increase the length of your walk. Don't initiate too ambitious a routine all at once.

• Smaller dogs require less exercise and have less stamina. A six-pound Chihuahua can get used to a one-mile walk, but a three-pounder will likely only go half that distance.

• Don't exercise the dog in hot weather. In summer months, avoid the midday sun. Early mornings and early evenings are the best time for walking. Chis don't like icy, snowy days either. Blizzards in Mexico are rare and unpopular!

- When you see signs of fatigue in your Chihuahua, pick him up and carry him home. Cool him off if necessary with cool water or a damp washcloth.

- Offer clean, fresh water during exercise and play sessions. Bring along a water bottle if you decide to take your Chi on a hike, long walk, or excursion to a beach or park.

- Keep your Chi on his leash and be extremely protective and proactive. While some well-trained Chihuahuas are fairly obedient when off leash, keep in mind that accidents can happen and you cannot predict how other dogs will behave around your tiny dog. Chihuahuas won't back down from a challenge, and four pounds of machismo won't prevent a big dog from picking up your dog and shaking him.

- Dry your dog off when you return home from a walk in inclement weather. A damp coat can lead to sickness. You may want to give your Chi a quick brush or a warm bath if he's been on the beach or at the park to remove any debris on his paws and from his coat.

Conformation is competitive for a popular breed like the Chihuahua. If you are interested in showing your Chi, let your breeder know so that he or she can help you choose a pup with award-winning potential.

Don't be fooled by their small size: Chihuahuas are active in AKC events such as conformation, agility, and obedience. Once your Chihuahua is fully grown, he can compete in any event you set your mind to.

• Always abide by laws and regulations in the areas you live or are visiting. Often dog restrictions are posted on signs at beaches and parks. Clean up after your dog and don't bring him to places where dogs are prohibited. In shore areas, dogs may be permitted only in the off-season or in the early morning or later evening hours.

CONFORMATION

Conformation is the formal name for dog shows, in which dogs compete to show how they best *conform* to the breed standard agreed upon and kept by the national parent club. When most people think of an AKC conformation event, the

Junior Scholarships

The American Kennel Club shows its commitment to supporting young people in their interest in purebred dogs by awarding thousands of dollars in scholarships to those competing in Junior Showmanship. The scholarships range from $1,000 to $5,000 and are based on a person's academic achievements and his or her history with purebred dogs. Learn more at www.akc.org/kids_juniors.

mental image is of a large all-breed dog show, such as any of the major competitions that are televised annually, such as the Westminster Kennel Club show in February or the AKC's National Championship show in December. In fact, there are over 2,500 dog shows held annually in the United States, most of which are many times smaller than the ones we see on television. Dog shows in the United States date back over a hundred years but today are more popular than ever.

With their big-dog air of self-importance and their winning dispositions, Chihuahuas are extremely popular in the show ring. For many dogs and owners, it's a win-win situation. The dogs love the opportunity to be around other good-looking Chihuahuas where they can strut their stuff for their owners and for the judge, and owners love the time spent with their dogs and the chance to meet other Chi lovers and owners. Dog shows usually attract lots of spectators, and the Chihuahua ring is always a popular gathering place. What better way to impress the public with all of the good characteristics of the Chihuahua than to exhibit your beautiful, well-trained, and happily socialized dog for all to see!

Visit a dog show in your area before deciding on whether or not to show your own dog. Dog shows are great places to meet friendly Chihuahua enthusiasts who have a wealth of knowledge to share. As long as you approach the handlers when they're not getting ready for the show ring, most will be more than happy to talk about their favorite topic: Chihuahuas. Visit the AKC website at www.akc.org or the Chihuahua Club of America website at www.chihuahuaclubofamerica.com to find local dog shows in your area.

If you're interested in getting involved with dog shows, contact a show breeder and let him or her know about your hopes before purchasing a dog. A show-quality puppy will cost more than a pet Chihuahua, but you're better off investing the time and money into a Chi that shows the potential of meeting the requirements of the breed standard. While it's fun to enter the ring with any dog, it's more fun to emerge from the competition with a ribbon and to eventually earn the title of Champion. And remember, the root purpose of dog shows is to promote the breeding of dogs that are as close to the breed standard as possible. As such, all show dogs must remain unaltered, that is, not spayed or neutered. Learn more at www.akc.org/events/conformation.

PERFORMANCE EVENTS

Lots of brains and lots of energy go far in AKC performance events. While it's not as common to see a Chihuahua leaping over jumps as it is to see a Golden Retriever or a Border Collie, there are still many Chis out there making a name for the breed in obedience and agility trials. Chihuahua owners attest that there's nothing more rewarding than training this little dog to compete in various AKC trials and events. Chihuahuas regard their much-loved owners as the center of their universe, and there's nothing better than partnering with your canine soulmate, regardless of whether you win or lose.

Obedience

Since the 1930s, the AKC has sponsored obedience trials, which can be held in conjunction with a dog show or as an independent event. A handler in an obedience trial must take his or her dog through a set of exercises which are scored by a judge. The exercises utilize the basic commands that all owners teach their dogs, such as *sit*, *down*, *stay*, *heel*, and *come*. There are three levels of obedience trials,

Your Best Amigo

There are many possibilities for you and your Chihuahua to get involved in your community. Your responsibility as a dog owner begins with investing in your Chihuahua's education, from home-schooling to training classes, hopefully progressing on to the AKC S.T.A.R. Puppy® and Canine Good Citizen® Programs. If you decide to step into the AKC world of organized events, you may discover that you and your Chihuahua love the thrill of competing in an agility trial or exhibiting at a dog show. Perhaps you're motivated by the possibility of visiting children at the Ronald McDonald House, recovering soldiers at a veterans' hospital, or elderly folk at a nursing home and want to pursue therapy work. Whatever you choose to do with your Chihuahua, he will prove to be a willing and talented participant, always ready to share his good looks, intelligence, obedience skills, affection, and, of course, that sweet temperament. Make the most of your Chihuahua and you will have the best friend you've ever had for many years to come.

each one progressively more difficult: Novice, Open, and Utility; and there are specific titles available at the different levels. Beyond the Novice level, the dogs are required to perform off leash, and in the Utility level, only hand signals are allowed. Dogs must be at least six months of age to compete.

Chihuahuas do not typically win over the ubiquitous Border Collie at an obedience trial, but they have indeed come home with High in Trial awards, outperforming dozens of the regular contenders. There's nothing a Chihuahua and his owner can't do when they are committed. Interested in getting involved in obedience? Visit www.akc.org/events/obedience.

Agility

A more recent phenomenon, agility trials have quickly become AKC's most popular performance event because they are great fun for the dog and handler and very exciting for spectators. With high jumps, tunnels, seesaws, weave poles, dog walks, and A-frames, agility trials are essentially obstacle courses for the dog and handler. Like obedience, agility is open to all purebred dogs and mixed breeds, both altered or unaltered. There are three classes in standard agility: Novice, Open, and Agility Excellent; and there is also a second variety known as Jumpers. To accommodate the various heights of dogs, there are five height divisions. Chihuahuas, of course, are in the lowest height division.

In addition to AKC agility, members of the Chihuahua Club of America also compete at trials hosted by the Teacup Dogs Agility Association (www.k9tdaa .com), which hosts events for small dogs. The distance between obstacles is

Did You Know?

In agility, Chihuahuas truly can do anything, especially if they're trained like MACH 2 Maximillion, owned by Linda Chapler. In 2001, Max was the first of his breed to receive the Master Agility Champion title, the highest award available to a dog competing in agility.

shortened, and all of the equipment is scaled down in size so that Toy dogs can compete more successfully. As in AKC trials, the dogs are timed and a judge sets each course. There is also a Toy-dog-only trial held in Massachusetts by the Classic Toy Dog Club (www.classictoydogclub.org).

If you're interested in getting started in agility trials, AKC recommends that you take a training class for companion events that is geared to prepare students and their canine partners, instructing them on levels of competition, regulations for each class, titles you can earn, and how to train your dog to accomplish the required exercises. Visit the AKC website for more information at www.akc.org/events/agility. You can also find your local breed club through the Chihuahua Club of America's website, www.chihuahuaclubofamerica.com, to find out about training courses and upcoming events in your area.

The AKC Code of Sportsmanship

- Sportsmen respect the history, traditions, and integrity of the sport of pure-bred dogs.
- Sportsmen commit themselves to values of fair play, honesty, courtesy, and vigorous competition, as well as winning and losing with grace.
- Sportsmen refuse to compromise their commitment and obligation to the sport of purebred dogs by injecting personal advantage or consideration into their decisions or behavior.
- The sportsman judge judges only on the merits of the dogs and considers no other factors.
- The sportsman judge or exhibitor accepts constructive criticism.
- The sportsman exhibitor declines to enter or exhibit under a judge where it might reasonably appear that the judge's placements could be based on something other than the merits of the dogs.
- The sportsman exhibitor refuses to compromise the impartiality of a judge.
- The sportsman respects the American Kennel Club's bylaws, rules, regulations, and policies governing the sport of purebred dogs.
- Sportsmen find that vigorous competition and civility are not inconsistent and are able to appreciate the merit of their competition and the efforts of competitors.
- Sportsmen welcome, encourage, and support newcomers to the sport.
- Sportsmen will deal fairly with all those who trade with them.
- Sportsmen are willing to share honest and open appraisals of both the strengths and weaknesses of their breeding stock.
- Sportsmen spurn any opportunity to take personal advantage of positions offered or bestowed upon them.
- Sportsmen always consider as paramount the welfare of their dogs.
- Sportsmen refuse to embarrass the sport, the American Kennel Club, or themselves while taking part in the sport.

Once your Chi has mastered all of the basic commands required in obedience, passing the Canine Good Citizen test is a snap.

AKC Rally®

Rally is the newest performance event in the world of AKC sports and is based on the rally style of car racing. Handlers must lead their dogs through a series of stations, at which there is a sign that gives a direction such as "Stop and Down" or "Slow Forward from Sit." The dogs and handlers must complete each direction and move on to the next station. The entire course is timed, and the only rule is that the handlers may not touch their dogs. Rally is a fast-paced event that is less competitive and stringent than obedience or agility. It is geared toward pet owners who are interested in having fun with their dogs, rather than those bent on acquiring titles. To learn more about Rally, visit www.akc.org/events/rally.

THERAPY DOGS

Don't let the Chihuahua's size fool you—he has a heart as big as any dog, and he's more than willing to share it with the world around him. Therapy work gives dogs and owners a wonderful opportunity to touch the lives of people in need. Therapy dogs visit hospitals, retirement homes, and nursing homes to brighten the days of patients and elderly residents. Because the Chihuahua has been such a popular breed for so many years, many older folks become nostalgic about Chis they once owned or knew. Likewise, younger people are enchanted by the tiny dog they've seen in television commercials and movies. When trained and socialized, Chihuahuas can be the most endearing therapy dogs.

The first step toward getting involved in therapy work is to participate in the AKC's Canine Good Citizen® Program, which requires that the dog pass a ten-step test of basic skills and manners. A dog that passes the test receives a CGC certificate, which indicates the dog is reliable in public and is obedient to his owner. Most therapy-dog organizations require that dogs first pass the Canine Good Citizen test before becoming a certified therapy dog.

The second step is to register your dog with one of the therapy-dog organizations which assist dog owners with insurance, training, and contacts at various facilities that welcome therapy dogs. The AKC currently works with over fifty-five organizations, including Pet Partners® (www.petpartners.org), Therapy Dogs

Incorporated (www.therapydogs.com), Bright and Beautiful Therapy Dogs (www
.golden-dogs.org), Therapy Dogs International (www.tdi-dog.org), and Love on a
Leash (www.loveonaleash.org). The AKC also offers a Therapy Dog title (ThD) to
dogs whose owners have registered with one of these organizations and have successfully made fifty or more community-service visits. For more information, visit
www.akc.org/acktherapydog.

VIVA LA CHIHUAHUA

Getting involved with your Chihuahua can be as ambitious as conformation or
agility or as simple as daily walks around the block or playing fetch in the backyard. The important thing is to keep your Chihuahua active. No matter what you
choose to do with your Chihuahua, he will be overjoyed to simply spend some
one-on-one time with you, his favorite person. Keep your Chihuahua on his toes
throughout his life, and you will be rewarded with an energetic, intelligent, and
healthy four-pound dynamo.

It's never too late for your Chihuahua to get involved in therapy work.
Volunteer at a nursing home or
retirement community where your
Chi can simply sit in a comfortable
lap and lend emotional support.

At a Glance ...

Eager to get out of the backyard and into the competitive show ring? Conformation or the various
performance events of obedience, agility, or Rally may be a tempting choice for you and your Chi.
Learn more about these popular canine sports at www.akc.org.

. . . .

Therapy work is a great choice for outgoing, friendly Chihuahuas. If you want to share that tiny grin
and lovable personality with those in need, explore the world of therapy work. The first step is to
pass the AKC Canine Good Citizen® test.

. . . .

An active Chihuahua is a healthy Chihuahua. Keep your Chihuahua active and involved throughout his life, and you will be rewarded with a well-behaved, energetic friend that lives well into his
double digits.

Resources

BOOKS

The American Kennel Club's Meet the Breeds: Dog Breeds from A to Z, 2012 edition (Irvine, California: I-5 Press, 2011) The ideal puppy buyer's guide, this book has all you need to know about each breed currently recognized by the AKC.

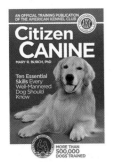

The Complete Dog Book, 20th edition (New York: Ballantine Books, 2006) This official publication of the AKC, first published in 1929, includes the complete histories and breed standards of 153 recognized breeds, as well as information on general care and the dog sport.

The Complete Dog Book for Kids (New York: Howell Book House, 1996) Specifically geared toward young people, this official publication of the AKC presents 149 breeds and varieties, as well as introductory owners' information.

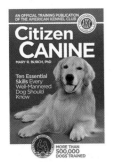

Citizen Canine: Ten Essential Skills Every Well-Mannered Dog Should Know by Mary R. Burch, PhD (Freehold, New Jersey: Kennel Club Books, 2010) This official AKC publication is the definitive guide to the AKC's Canine Good Citizen® Program, recognized as the gold standard of behavior for dogs, with more than half a million dogs trained.

DOGS: The First 125 Years of the American Kennel Club (Freehold, New Jersey: Kennel Club Books, 2009) This official AKC publication presents an authoritative, complete history of the AKC, including detailed information not found in any other volume.

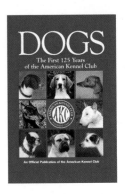

Dog Heroes of September 11th: A Tribute to America's Search and Rescue Dogs, 10th anniversary edition, by Nona Kilgore Bauer (Freehold, New Jersey: Kennel Club Books, 2011) A publication to salute the canines that served in the recovery missions following the September 11th attacks, this book serves as a lasting tribute to these noble American heroes.

The Original Dog Bible: The Definitive Source for All Things Dog, 2nd edition, by Kristin Mehus-Roe (Irvine, California: I-5 Press, 2009) This 831-page magnum opus includes more than 250 breed profiles, hundreds of color photographs, and a wealth of information on every dog topic imaginable—thousands of practical tips on grooming, training, care, and much more.

PERIODICALS

American Kennel Club Gazette

Every month since 1889, serious dog fanciers have looked to the *AKC Gazette* for authoritative advice on training, showing, breeding, and canine health. Each issue includes the breed columns section, written by experts from the respective breed clubs. Only available electronically.

AKC Family Dog

This is a bimonthly magazine for the dog lover whose special dog is "just a pet." Helpful tips, how-tos, and features are written in an entertaining and reader-friendly format. It's a lifestyle magazine for today's busy families who want to enjoy a rewarding, mutually happy relationship with their canine companions.

Dog Fancy

The world's most widely read dog magazine, *Dog Fancy* celebrates dogs and the people who love them. Each monthly issue includes info on cutting-edge medical developments, health and fitness (with a focus on prevention, treatment, and natural therapy), behavior and training, travel and activities, breed profiles and dog news, issues and trends for purebred and mixed-breed dog owners. The magazine informs, inspires, and entertains while promoting responsible dog ownership. Throughout its more than forty-year history, *Dog Fancy* has garnered numerous honors, including being named the Best All-Breed Magazine by the Dog Writers Association of America.

Dogs in Review

For more than fifteen years, *Dogs in Review* has showcased the finest dogs in the United States and from around the world. The emphasis has always been on strong content, with input from distinguished breeders, judges, and handlers worldwide. This global perspective distinguishes this monthly publication from its competitors—no other North American dog-show magazine gathers together so many international experts to enlighten and entertain its readership.

Dogs World Annual

Dog World (formerly *Dogs USA*) is an annual lifestyle magazine published by the editors of *Dog Fancy* that covers all aspects of the dog world: culture, art, history, travel, sports, and science. It also profiles breeds to help prospective owners choose the best dogs for their future needs, such as a potential show champion, super service dog, great pet, or competitive star.

Natural Dog

Natural Dog is the magazine dedicated to giving a dog a natural lifestyle. From nutritional choices to grooming to dog-supply options, this publication helps readers make the transition from traditional to natural methods. The magazine also explores the array of complementary treatments available for today's dogs: acupuncture, massage, homeopathy, aromatherapy, and much more. *Natural*

Dog appears as an annual publication and also as the flip side of *Dog Fancy* magazine four times a year (in February, May, August, and November).

Puppies USA

Also from the editors of *Dog Fancy*, this annual magazine offers essential information for all new puppy owners. *Puppies USA* is lively and informative, including advice on general care, nutrition, grooming, and training techniques for all puppies, whether purebred or mixed breed, adopted, rescued, or purchased. In addition, it offers family fun through quizzes, contests, and much more. An extensive breeder directory is included.

WEBSITES

www.akc.org

The American Kennel Club (AKC) website is an excellent starting point for researching dog breeds and learning about puppy care. The site lists hundreds of breeders, along with basic information about breed selection and basic care. The site also has links to the national breed club of every AKC-recognized breed; breed-club sites offer plenty of detailed breed information, as well as lists of member breeders. In addition, you can find the AKC National Breed Club Rescue List at www.akc.org/breeds/rescue.cfm. If looking for purebred puppies, go to www.puppybuyerinfo.com for AKC classifieds and parent-club referrals.

www.dogchannel.com

Powered by *Dog Fancy*, Dog Channel is "the website for dog lovers," where hundreds of thousands of visitors each month find extensive information on breeds, training, health and nutrition, puppies, care, activities, and more. Interactive features include forums, Dog College, games, and Club Dog, a free club where dog lovers can create blogs for their pets and earn points to buy products. Dog Channel is the one-stop site for all things dog.

www.meetthebreeds.com

The official website of the AKC Meet the Breeds® event, hosted by the American Kennel Club in the Jacob Javits Center in New York City in the fall. The first Meet the Breeds event took place in 2009. The website includes information on every recognized breed of dog and cat, alphabetically listed, as well as the breeders, demonstration facilitators, sponsors, and vendors participating in the annual event.

AKC AFFILIATES

The **AKC Museum of the Dog**, established in 1981, is located in St. Louis, Missouri, and houses the world's finest collection of art devoted to the dog. Visit www.museumofthedog.org.

The **AKC Humane Fund** promotes the joy and value of responsible and productive pet ownership through education, outreach, and grant-making. Monies raised may fund grants to organizations that teach responsible pet ownership; provide for the health and well-being of all dogs; and preserve and celebrate the human-animal bond and the evolutionary relationship between dogs and humankind. Go to www.akchumanefund.org.

The **American Kennel Club Companion Animal Recovery (CAR) Corporation** is dedicated to reuniting lost microchipped and tattooed pets with their owners. AKC CAR maintains a permanent-identification database and provides lifetime recovery services 24 hours a day, 365 days a year, for all animal species. Millions of pets are enrolled in the program, which was established in 1995. Visit www.akccar.org.

The **American Kennel Club Canine Health Foundation (AKC CHF), Inc.** is the largest foundation in the world to fund canine-only health studies for purebred and mixed-breed dogs. More than $22 million has been allocated in research funds to more than 500 health studies conducted to help dogs live longer, healthier lives. Go to www.akcchf.org.

AKC PROGRAMS

The **Canine Good Citizen Program (CGC)** was established in 1989 and is designed to recognize dogs that have good manners at home and in the community. This rapidly growing, nationally recognized program stresses responsible dog ownership for owners and basic training and good manners for dogs. All dogs that pass the ten-step Canine Good Citizen test receive a certificate from the American Kennel Club. Go to www.akc.org/events/cgc.

The **AKC S.T.A.R. Puppy Program** is designed to get dog owners and their puppies off to a good start and is aimed at loving dog owners who have taken the time to attend basic obedience classes with their puppies. After completing a six-week training course, the puppy must pass the AKC S.T.A.R. Puppy test, which evaluates Socialization, Training, Activity, and Responsibility. Go to www.akc.org/starpuppy.

The **AKC Therapy Dog** program recognizes all American Kennel Club dogs and their owners who have given their time and helped people by volunteering as a therapy dog-and-owner team. The AKC Therapy Dog program is an official American Kennel Club title awarded to dogs that have worked to improve the lives of the people they have visited. The AKC Therapy Dog title (AKC ThD) can be earned by dogs that have been certified by recognized therapy dog organizations. For more information, visit www .akc.org/akctherapydog.

Index

AMERICAN KENNEL CLUB®

Advocating for the purebred dog as a family companion, advancing canine health and well-being, working to protect the rights of all dog owners and promoting responsible dog ownership, the **American Kennel Club:**

Sponsors more than **22,000 sanctioned events** annually including conformation, agility, obedience, rally, tracking, lure coursing, earthdog, herding, field trial, hunt test, and coonhound events

Features a **10-step Canine Good Citizen® program** that rewards dogs who have good manners at home and in the community

Has reunited more than **400,000** lost pets with their owners through the AKC Companion Animal Recovery - visit **www.akccar.org**

Created and supports the AKC Canine Health Foundation, which funds research projects using the more than **$22 million** the AKC has donated since 1995 - visit **www.akcchf.org**

Joins **animal lovers** through education, outreach and grant-making via the AKC Humane Fund - visit **www.akchumanefund.org**

We're more than champion dogs. We're the dog's champion.

www.akc.org